# PRAYER POWER

*by*
*J. Moulton*
*Thomas*

*A Key-Word Book*
*Word Books, Publisher*
*Waco, Texas*

*To "Andy"*
*Mother of our four sons*
*and peerless prayer partner*

# contents

## acknowledgments

I am indebted to those
whose words I have quoted
and acknowledged. I am just as
indebted for quotations by those
whose names I have forgotten.

# foreword

It gives me real joy to write the foreword for this book by Moulton Thomas, whom I have known in Christian fellowship for many years.

So few have written about the place of group prayer in the renewal of the church, that I consider it a most timely contribution to renewal and evangelism which are among our most relevant and needed emphases in our day. The theme of the book is brought out in a quotation that he uses: "Love does not consist in gazing at each other, but in looking together in the same direction."

In the 60s, the church brought us the New Morality with its empty promises, as well as horizontal social activism, not often undergirded with prayer. Neither of these emphases, which were relevant at the time, seem to have satisfied the profound hunger in people for the basic realities of our faith. These, "Mo" Thomas has spelled out in highlights.

I particularly like his emphasis on the triangle. The prayer power of the church does consist in "trialogue" rather than dialogue. Trialogue is the heart of prayer, where, in Jesus Christ, God is the apex of the triangle, and we, the people of God—whether in marriage, business, church, government, or international relationships—are at the base of that triangle. No great breakthroughs can take place unless men and women are not only dialoguing with each other, but listening to God's Holy Spirit, and, in community, receive his direction.

There is, on the reverse of the Great Seal of the United States, a pyramid, with the eye of God at the top. Written above are the words *Annuit Coeptis* which mean, "He watches over our beginnings." Underneath is written, "A new order for the ages." This was the vision

11

of the founding fathers who wrote the Declaration of Independence and the Constitution. This should be the base on which we continue to build. People around the world look to us for help, yet, the American dream is a hollow shell without the prayer power described in this book.

His chapters, "Prayer Power for Families," "Prayer Power for the Clergy," "Prayer Power for the Church" are particularly effective because they emphasize the mystery of group power.

In this Bicentennial year, it is my warm hope that this book will be widely read and will undergird the growing number of Americans who are engaged in, or wish to be engaged in, personal and group prayer all over the nation.

Someone has said, very truly, "there is nothing so dangerous as a Christian, just off his knees." I am convinced that prayer is a force that can be utilized only by those who love and trust God, and who let the stream of their life-purpose run along in the stream of His great will.

HELEN SMITH SHOEMAKER

# introduction

*"Be prepared to make a defense
to any one who calls you to account
for the hope that is in you"* (1 Pet. 3:15).

WHENEVER OIL and gas resources, physical energy and electrical power are in short supply, it is *good news* that prayer power is inexhaustible. The *bad news* is that this divine energy is largely untapped by the clergy, as well as by the laity.

Prayer power is more than powerful answers to our petitions. In fact, in this book we are not concerned with getting anything, whether a miracle of healing, a job, having our spirits lifted in ecstasy or victory over death. Most of us do not feel we are praying unless we get thrills. Oswald Chambers in *My Utmost for His Highest* says, "that this is the intensest form of spiritual selfishness."

Joyful gifts often happen in the context of liberating prayer, for the Father does have gifts that pass men's understanding. Here, however, we will center upon a largely unknown experience for communicants of most churches: the difference it makes when a few persons, committed to Jesus Christ, realize together the power and love of his presence, seeking only to let the Holy Spirit make us into a fellowship

prayer
individual
and
corporate

13

available to him for the resurrection of his Body, the church.

Two aspects of prayer are familiar to us—individual prayer and liturgical or corporate prayer. For individual prayer, Jesus said, "Go into your room and shut the door and pray to your Father who is in secret" (Matt. 6:6). To the corporate body, Jesus said, "Do this in remembrance of me" (Luke 22:19, Phillips). So with clergy and congregation, "with Angels and Archangels and with all the company of heaven," we do praise him.

A third aspect of prayer, the informal fellowship of a small group, is also apostolic. Jesus said, "Where two or three are gathered in my name, there am I in the midst of them" (Matt. 18:20). He sent them out two by two in his name. Three on a mountain top beheld

*the missing link*

his glory. A small group of twelve were to be with him so that as they loved one another the world would know they were his disciples. And near the end of Jesus' life, he said in gratitude to this small group, "You are those who have continued with me in my trials" (Luke 22:28).

Paul preached to crowds as Jesus did. But it was upon the responsible shoulders and responsive spirits of a few in prayer at Ephesus, a few at Philippi, at Colossae, and at Corinth that Paul counted for the enriching of his own spirit and the undergirding of all future activity.

My hope is that this brief work will be of assistance in the continuation of the renewing life. The book and division titles arose from a series of weekend workshops on prayer power in parishes of ten Eastern states over five years.

I am deeply grateful to the clergy who, in inviting me, gave me the opportunity to see hundreds of their parishioners discover, individually, new life in Jesus Christ, and by the miracle of his love, in prayer, change houses into homes, occupations into vocations, and "church work" into Christian community. This took place with the development of small study-prayer groups.

Helpful critics of this manuscript were at first apprehensive because my orientation is Anglican (though with a Roman Catholic grandfather and Methodist grandmother) and I use terms like *vestry, rector, diocese,* and *prayer book.* They feared that prospective readers might decide that the contents applied only to Episcopalians. First, I replied that the material has been forged at conferences and workshops with clergy and laity of Congregational, Presbyterian, Methodist, Baptist, and Roman Catholic, as well as Episcopal churches. Second, our terms have counterparts in each communion, and these, I am sure, can be so translated in the reader's mind. Third, I would be happy if Episcopalians derived benefit because, with Canon Jack Clough, Ontario, I agree: "If the Anglican Communion doesn't fall on its knees, it will soon fall flat on its face."

During a battle in World War II, a chaplain crawled to where a soldier lay dying. "Do you want me to have a prayer with you?"

The soldier replied, "But I don't belong to your church."

"Yes, but you do belong to my God."

Fellowships of prayer with men, women, and college students of all faiths have made me certain that we do belong to the same God and can rejoice together in the fellowship of his Holy Spirit.

J. MOULTON THOMAS

# Prevailing Power

Lord, what a change within us one short hour
Spent in Thy Presence doth prevail to make!
What heavy burdens from our bosoms take.
What parched grounds revive as with a shower.
We kneel, how weak, we arise, how full of power.
Why, therefore, should we do ourselves this wrong,
Or others, that we are not always strong;
That we are ever overborne with care,
That we should ever weak or heartless be,
Anxious or troubled, when with us in prayer,
And joy and strength and courage are with thee?

ARCHBISHOP TRENCH (1807–1886)

# 1

# a Christian autobiography

*Prayer is not real until it becomes
part of my autobiography.*

ON THE LEVEL of ideas, it is easy to interrelate
with people for a long time and yet not really
know them. On the level of joint activity
(church, civic, social) it is easy to use a task
or an endeavor as a shield against familiarity or
intimacy. We hold others at arm's length, main-
taining a façade that is a bit defensive because
in certain spots we are vulnerable. We defend
ourselves by hiding behind ideas, activity, or
silences. Clergy hide from other clergy and
from their parishioners. Wives and husbands
hide from each other and from their children.

However, on the level of commitment to
Jesus Christ, our relationships are distinguished
by a clear and transparent quality. When others know me (when I am honest about my
needs and they honest about theirs), we see
each other in a brand-new way. This does not
happen simply because "misery loves company"
(because it really doesn't), but because we are
honestly sharing one another's burdens.

This is not to urge that "we hang all our

how
we
hide

dirty linen on the line." It is a plea for each of us to admit that there are, probably, a few people God wants us to begin with, whom we have worked with and cared for, but not cared enough.

In groups which might use this book, members already know something about one another: size of family, place of employment, political or athletic interests. We may even know some of one another's hurts and problems, but do we know one another as Christians? Here are four questions that have been used to break down barriers in small groups of Christian people who wish to develop new relationships and find prayer power.

1. What were the childhood influences that made my Christian faith strong, weak, or indifferent?
2. What was my understanding of "confirmation" or "joining the church" at the time?
3. Which adult experiences have made faith in Christ less real or more real?
4. In what one area do I need God's grace?

how
we
discover

In meeting with new clergy and laity, or with those whom I have known superficially in social or church activities, my own mini-autobiography has included the following basic items.

1. My childhood could not have been happier. I hold warm memories of supportive, loving relationships. Father, who had considered the ministry, became a lawyer. He was keen to further the church's mission—personal, parochial, or worldwide.

Before his funeral, one of his friends said to me, "The difference between your father and me is that, although I go to church, he carried part of it, and it gave him more than I have found." My father was the kind of layman every clergyman hopes for but seldom finds. (I never found one like him.)

My mother, though a leader in parish affairs, found such joy in Sunday worship that all during the week it lingered and gave our home a unique beauty. Her copy of Baillie's *Diary of Private Prayer* had to be rebound after thirty years of use. The underlining, attached clippings, and her own handwritten expressions of faith make it now, for me, her spiritual bequest.

Mother and father together found strength in prayer which was not a duty but a natural response to their faith in God's love. I remember as a small child entering their bedroom unannounced and finding them on their knees beside the bed. I tiptoed out and have kept this memory as one of my choicest.

My grandfather lived with us. He was keen, witty, and a lover of the works of Shakespeare, Burns, and Scott. Gangrene had cost him—at age seventy-seven—the loss of both legs. How he took his affliction with cheerfulness and trust! I was an only child, but grandfather adequately made up for the lack of sibling relationships. I was his only grandson and his namesake. His love was rich, and I think he spoiled me a bit! These three loving persons gave me a creative and secure home life.

2. My understanding of confirmation (joining the church), at thirteen, consisted of two things: first, preparation; second, the service. Instruction included the meaning of the creed, the Lord's Prayer, and the Ten Commandments. Happily this was more than memorizing; my teacher was a saintly man to whom these spiri-

tual foundations were exciting and true. I anticipated the "laying on of hands"—not so much the bishop's but Christ's reaching down through the centuries to me. An incident in the service interrupted my reverie. The bishop's ring had slipped around so that the seal was on the inside of his palm. It descended on my head with such force that it shattered the pretty image of Christ's hands. At the same time, it did make a memorable impression!

3. My adult experiences of closeness to God or remoteness from him have been many. These two extremes met for the first time when I was a sophomore at Princeton University.

Sam Shoemaker had preached in the college chapel that morning. As was customary, in the evening, students were invited to meet with the speaker. The directness of this winsome Marylander, in the morning, meant that the lounge of Murray Dodge Hall was jammed. I could only find space looking through the banisters on the steps halfway to the second floor.

At the conclusion he asked, "Have you fellows given your lives to God to be used by him?" It took me two months to understand and to answer.

the
question

For about a week I could answer yes, trying to justify myself by imagined virtue. Then the last five words came again and again and dared me to face the adventure that lay just ahead.

"To be used by him!" What? Give God a signed blank check over the future? But I realized that there would be no Christian future unless I checked the sub-Christian past and present. This included willingness to admit to the dean that I had broken the honor system and cheated on an exam. It would also mean being willing to take the initiative to bridge a half-satisfying relationship that had recently developed with my father.

Above all it meant the fear of having to scrap the plans for my life-work. What if God wanted me in his ministry? Perish the thought! To wear a round collar? To look like I was going the wrong way the rest of my life? But how true it is that if you fight with your conscience and *lose,* then you win.

After eight weeks of sleepless nights, of distractions from studies, and a great sense of aloneness, "pride ruled my will" and made me miserable.

Finally came my yes to God. "God, if you can possibly use a guy like me, O.K." A healthy conviction of sin led to a healthy release and freedom. I then knew what "being born again" meant and what it felt like. I had known the support of an earthly father; I now knew the greater love of an everlasting Father. I had known about Jesus as friend and teacher but now as redeemer, bringing peace and freedom. I had had vague conceptions of the Holy Ghost but now he became, with joy, the indwelling Lord—Holy Guest—to correct and to direct, "into all truth."

I waited on my knees. What would be the Holy Spirit's first guidance? It was not heroic or spectacular—quite simple and very practical, "Now get some sleep, you need it." I thought of the episode when Jesus raised from the dead the daughter of Jairus and said, "Give her something to eat!" (Luke 8:55, LB).

*guidance*

The next morning on the way to breakfast I stopped downstairs to pick up Dave. He, too, had been wrestling with his answer to Sam's question.

"You've done it," he said.

"What?" I asked.

"You've given your life to Christ? You don't look like you did last night."

"Yes I have, and thank God I don't feel like I did last night. Even the wallpaper looked different this morning."

Dave said, "I can't hold out. Will you pray with me? I want to make my decision."

We knelt and a fellowship of prayer for two began. Our Lord was in our midst as he had promised. It was my introduction to prayer power.

That afternoon I told the dean the whole story. He said he would have to refer it to the senior council. Ten days later he called me in. "Mo, you can stay. The council decided that this might be the most important thing you will ever learn in college." And it was!

restitution

At the next vacation, a new bridge was built with my father. I could look ahead and agree with John: "We are God's children now; it does not yet appear what we shall be" (1 John 3:2). Adventure!

Sam didn't know where his question had led me until I saw him a year later, and told him.

4. In small groups in which this questionnaire has been used, my needs of God's grace have differed from time to time. Here are some that I recall:

To love a person who seemed to block spiritual advances in a parish and opposed me!

To stop using people for "church work" at the expense of changing them.

To get through being hurt by those I love, who neglect or renounce the Christian faith.

To get over being sentimental with parishioners: talking of Christ, but standing in his way. How often I have needed to recall the advice of an old clergyman at my ordination: "Remember your job is to draw aside the curtains. Reveal Christ on his cross, but don't forget to hide yourself in the folds of that curtain."

The use of these four questions is one way to remove ignorance and build confidence in a small group. With this start, we discover that, as important as ideas and activities still are, something very real has been taking place. We see areas where we may, in a new way, appreciate, understand, and pray more intelligently with and for each other.

*redeemed
from
estrangement*

Prayer fellowship is one answer to the longing in these lines:

> This is our poverty, Lord,
> We do not belong to each other,
> Or serve one another.
> We each go his own way
> And do not care for our neighbor.
> Oh, Lord, redeem us
> From this estrangement!

When Jesus ministered to a blind man, he touched his eyes once. The man's sight began to come back. "What do you see?"

*the
second
touch*

"I see men as trees, walking."

Then he touched them again, "Now I see things clearly."

Our view of one another, our knowledge of one another, can become distorted. We see men as interesting or boring, as "our kind" or foreigners, friends or enemies, black or white. When we let Jesus open our eyes to the truth about ourselves and others, we see clearly. We recognize men as brothers in Jesus Christ.

# 2

# gospel, theology, religion

*I know who I am because
I know whose I am.*

IF THERE IS ONE thing that characterizes the apostles, Paul, and the evangelists Matthew, Mark, Luke, and John, it is their certainty about the gospel.

They agreed that Jesus lived in a certain place and time, that he was crucified, that he died, and that God raised him from the dead. They were certain that God the Father, because of his love, had revealed himself through his Son. They were certain that though there were countless ideas of God, Jesus Christ was God's idea of himself. They were certain that God the Holy Spirit had also come in a body **Christian** of reborn men and women. They were certain **certainty** that they (his body, the church) were commissioned to take the Good News to the ends of the earth and to the end of time.[1]

Today the claim of certainty is suspect. It is often called simplistic. In some circles, questioning, searching, and *not* finding seems more intellectually respectable. Those who prefer to be like Tantalus, with a thirst that is never quenched, we leave to their own sophisticated agnosticism. We believe that most people, when they seek, expect to find. Goethe said, "Tell me your certainties; I have enough doubts of my own."

J. B. Phillips writes:

> To many, somewhat depressed Christians today, there comes, at times, the feeling that they are clinging to an interpretation of life which they believe to be the truth, but which the world around regards as merely one of many interpretations.
>
> This is an unnecessarily depressing attitude, for the Christian is, by faith, reaching out and touching the real world.
>
> To the early Christian, it was a faith which gave their lives their astonishing quality.
>
> And to us (once we accept Christ as the planned focus of God in history)
>
> 1. Our faith becomes a certainty.
> 2. We know what sort of person God is.
> 3. What kind of plan He is attempting to work out.
> 4. How we can be made whole.
> 5. How in the Fellowship of the Holy Spirit, with others, the world can be made whole.[2]

What is this gospel that Christians are so certain about? It is not a set of theological propositions that we must prove or approve. The gospel is not the creed. It is not the Ten Commandments. It is not that men ought to love one another. The gospel is not an *ought*. The gospel is an *is*. The gospel is not a princi-

the
gospel

27

ple, but a Person. "It is the Word in action, and the Word is Jesus: the word Love."[3]

With no uncertainty, Studdert-Kennedy wrote:

I bet my life on Beauty, Truth,
And Love.—not abstract, but Incarnate Truth,
Not Beauty's passing shadow, but Itself
Its very Self made Flesh. Love realized.
I bet my life on Christ; Christ crucified.[4]

Bishop John Robinson has written:

The message of the New Testament is that we have no need to wait until the end of history, or even the end of our lives, to be up against God's last Word, for, in Jesus Christ, we meet Him in such a way that there is nothing more for Him to say. God is so radically concerned about man on earth, that He became man Himself.[5]

The gospel is the good news that the "Ground of our Being" came on our ground, and his first name is Jesus. Crucified and risen, he is our eternal contemporary. He joins us to his other friends by prayer, in a brand-new relationship called the fellowship of the Holy Spirit. In fellowship with others, he changes us. He changes our use of money and possessions, our homes, our attitudes. He changes superiority and inferiority into mutual trust. He changes despair into hope, and sorrow into joy, when first of all, the necessary change takes place in me and in you. Paul—writing of the joyful relationship with the disciples in Macedonia—tells us how it came about: "First they gave themselves to the Lord and to us by the will of God" (2 Cor. 8:5).

This is the gospel today, because it was so 2000 years ago in Palestine. We recall that Jesus called men to himself. He did not call them to a philosophy, nor to a cause, nor to a special work. He said, "Come to me," not "Come to my Bible," not "Come to my friends the saints," not "Come to my mother." They may all be in the developing picture, but he said, "Come to me."

*come to me!*

Andrew met him and introduced his brother, Peter. Philip brought Nathaniel. James and John joined the group. A woman of Samaria met him at a well. He forgave her her adultery. She carelessly left her water pot, ran back to town to tell her patrons of this man. They came and met him, and persuaded him to stay two days, and when he left they said, "It is no longer because of your words that we believe, for we have heard for ourselves, and we know that this is indeed the Savior of the world" (John 4:42).

In Athens, Paul, speaking of the altar dedicated to the unknown god, said, "Him whom you ignorantly worship I declare to you, Jesus, crucified, risen and alive" (Acts 17:23–24, paraphrased). Yes, the gospel in Palestine, Greece, Rome and Britain was the living Lord, Jesus Christ. And today the gospel still is Jesus at the heart of a man or woman, at the heart of changed human relationships. This is the gospel in the midst of any perplexity and any society, "the message for our mess-age."

Bishop John Hines said, "The gospel is what God *has already done* in Jesus, in history and in me; a new life, a new freedom, a new order of unseen values, a new personal relationship with God and each other, and a new order of growing relationships by the grace of God."

To the Ephesians, St. Paul wrote, "Having the eyes of your hearts enlightened, that you may know what is the hope to which he has called you, what are the riches of his glorious inheritance in the saints" (Eph. 1:18).

**Christian power**

The Christian power (the power of God's love and the power to love) is a matter of personal concern as well as a matter of intellectual understanding. When I was chaplain on Trinity College campus, theological questions were brought to me by students and faculty members. "How can one pray to a God he cannot see?" "How is God a loving Father with so much suffering?" Their inquiries were sincere, and I would answer as best I could. But, sooner or later, I would suggest that, for the time being, we put these theological questions on a shelf so that the intellectual concern could be dealt with *after* the personal was seen and faced with Jesus Christ. These personal problems or questions ranged from disquieting relationships with parents, roommates, and dates, to academic failure and expulsion. They had to do with guilt and sometimes with dislike of themselves. Faculty members had problems with wives and other faculty members.

**campus dis-ease**

Dr. E. Stanley Jones listed four basic causes of campus dis-ease. Not one of them is an intellectual problem; they are all personal—laziness, loneliness, lust, and lack of purpose. This personal disquiet is hidden beneath family tension, public confusion, social prejudices, and racial unrest. On a CBS broadcast in 1972, Eric Sevareid said: "College students are coming to discover that personal problems are harder to solve than social, racial, or economic problems."

What is theology? What is religion? Very

simply theology is any philosophy that includes
a god or that denies God. The ultimate goal of
theology is to arrive at a reasonable QED, that
is, an answer to the question, What can satisfy
my mind? The Christian religion, however, is
man's *whole* relationship with the Christian
God. Christian theology says, I believe *that*
God is a father, *that* God came in Jesus, *that*
the Holy Spirit guides, and *that* there is resurrection. Christian religion says, I believe *in*
God whom I know as Almighty Father, *in* Jesus whom I know as my Redeemer, and *in* the
Holy Spirit who guides, corrects, and directs.

theology:
believing
that

The word *believe* comes to us via Old and
Middle English from the Indo-European root
*Leubh*, meaning "to care" or "to desire." In
Old and Middle English the prefix *be* means
"entirely" or "overwhelming." To *believe in*
God is "to love him entirely" and "to be loved
overwhelmingly."[6] So personal is this experience that in the eucharist we can say "that he
may dwell in us and we in him."

to
believe

Whereas the ultimate goal of theology is to
satisfy the reason (perhaps one-third of a
man), the goal of religion is a man on his
knees. Mind, body, will, memory, hopes, and
plans all devoted to God and given back to
God to be used by him and in communion
with him. We must not forget that Paul's and
John's and Peter's theology, that is, what they
believed *about* God, resulted from their religion
—their experience with Jesus as friend, teacher,
as crucified and as the risen Christ in the fellowship of the Holy Spirit. They *hung their theology* on this certainty of being loved.

religion:
believing *in*

It is only from *within* the Christian experience that one could write: "Our theme is the
word of life. . . . we have seen it and bear

our testimony; we have declared to you the eternal life which dwelt with the Father and was made visible to us. . . . we write this in order that the joy of us all may be complete" (1 John 1:1–4, NEB).

Theology, therefore, must follow experience and not go before. What a pity if a man would have to be a theologian before he could know God!

We can see the difference between believing "that" something is true "about" God and believing "in" God. Mr. Brezhnev, in 1976, believes that democracy exists. He tried to stamp it out in Czechoslovakia, in Poland, and Hungary. He would demoralize us and undermine the USA, but if he flew to Washington and asked for asylum in order to experience freedom, we could then say that he believes *in* democracy: total commitment.

*In theology, God is my problem.* What proof will satisfy my mind of his existence: What is he like? I, personally, have many unanswered questions about God in theology, but *in religion, I am God's problem,* and his is greater than mine!

I found this quote: "The world's greatest problem is not man's but God's—not how man can get into God's outer space, but how he can get into man's inner space, to be man's friend and Savior." How can he persuade me to recognize his Love? How can he get me to open from the inside, the fast-closed door of my will? How can he set me free from captivity to my pride or my grief, my fear, my lust, my guilt, my self-pity, my prejudices and my false faces? How can he set me free enough to let me love my neighbor, love my family, yes, to love myself, and to bring new life to his church? In

short, his problem is how to move me from
B.C. confusion to A.D. discovery and grace. We
will see that prayer power is resurrection power.

It was the late Bishop Powell of Maryland
who once said, "Forming a statue from the
hardest granite is easy compared to God's task
of trying to melt the human heart."

We began by noting the physical energy
shortage of our day. This must be dealt with
by industry and government, with our cooperation, but here, we rejoice in the good news
which the church offers, and only the church
supplies, the inexhaustible prayer power of God
and his love.

B.C.
to
A.D.

# 3

# why pray at all?

*Prayer unites me with God*
*me with myself*
*me with you.*

MOST OF US, if we say our prayers, do so with varying degrees of reality and habit. We must admit that we Christians in general have not been known for our depth of spirituality, for the joyfulness of our faith, or for unselfconscious and informal prayer with one another. We may say that we are the reticent kind. It may well be that we are the ignorant kind or the uncommitted kind of Christian, and—for Episcopalians—this is usually true in spite of our familiarity with (or maybe because of our familiarity with) the Book of Common Prayer. We have *said* our prayers. We may yet have to learn to pray.

*prayer and praying*

The purpose of prayer is very simple: to afford a time and a place to be with God because we are his creatures and we need him, and, because love is interdependent and he needs us.

*I need God*

A psychologist once pointed out that to become a whole person an individual must have six basic needs fulfilled. Three are timeless; three are temporal. The first timeless necessity

*three timeless needs*

is that man must have an object outside himself around which to center his life, in order to bring in line his many-sidedness.

I remember, as a child, enjoying the weird sounds produced by a Victrola record through which I had drilled a hole one inch off-center, causing the record to wobble. One could still detect the song but with great disharmony. Men with confusions, conflicts, and defeats are running their lives off-center.

*object of devotion*

The second timeless need, if we would be whole, is for a work to accomplish, a cause to strive for, something challenging enough to absorb our energies and to sharpen our imaginations.

*goal*

Dr. Paul Tournier applies this need especially to today's youth.

> For the older generation, modern technical development was a passionate adventure of invention. To the younger generation, who receive this all ready-made, when they were still in the crib, it is like a too-easy gift: demoralizing. They look like no more than colorless tinsel, put around life. This generation is, basically, seeking a gift which ours has not been able to provide: a valid purpose for life.[1]

The third timeless need is for motivation. College deans and high school guidance counselors find many able students without the energy to meet their capabilities.

*motivation*

Frank Goble, president of Thomas Jefferson Research Center, says that a society cannot survive without a workable system of values.

"Yet how does one educate people to be moral, ethical and responsible? There's the rub.

Many scholars insist there is no way to teach morals; you can only teach *about* them. That is a way of saying humans can be taught *how* and *why* to follow a certain code of conduct, but nothing can make them do the right thing if they don't care to" [if not motivated].[2]

three
temporal
needs
for past
present
future

A person has three temporal needs. The first is for the present, the second is for the past, and the third is for the future. The essential for the present is survival: shelter, sustenance, and health. The essential for the past is how to deal with our memories and our failures. The essential for the future is guidance in decisions and confidence in meeting the unknown, whether the unknown is immediate or whether it is eternal.

before
psychology

The Christian believer finds that long before psychology was a serious study, Jesus Christ pointed the way to become a whole person in each of these six areas. In the few words of the Lord's Prayer, he shows that prayer is the secret key to the meaning of human wholeness.

our
father

First, for the timeless need of an object of devotion to bring our chaotic divisions into harmony, our true center is not some other person, not our unknowable, or our cosmic energy "who art in heaven," but "our Father, hallowed be your name." In the confusion of many people about their identity, as a twice born Christian, I know *who* I am, because I know *Whose* I am. I am a child of a heavenly Father who for me sent Jesus, for me he was crucified, and rose from the tomb, and for me, by water and the Holy Spirit made me a member of his continuing Body, here and hereafter. What an identity! Not just for me but for all men. What gratitude it generates! What "ground of being" to stand on! What a gospel to stand for!

With that discovery, we find that we are not looking for God, we know that in Jesus Christ, he has been here looking for us, and he has found us. First he has *found us out:* exposed our defenses, punctured our egos, and spotlighted our moral and spiritual poverty (pointing out "the one thing thou lackest").

Second, he *found for us* adequate forgiveness and freedom from the past, communion with him and with others in the present, and the sure and certain hope of our resurrection. What a Father! That is what the Good News is all about. From then on "his service is perfect freedom."

Our Lord's direction for a cause to accomplish was "thy kingdom come on earth." This cause never runs out of possibilities for the minds, or the wills, or the energies and the abilities of every last man and woman to the ends of the earth. The kingdom of God is the kingdom of right relationships, not only between men, as is the aim of psychology and sociology, but between God and a man and all men with God, and with each other, through him.

**your kingdom**

In the third place, for motivation in the face of monotony, disappointments, and failures, Jesus said to pray for God's creative will, *his* will power, "thy will be done." Often, a person with burdens too hard to bear says with a sigh, "I suppose I must accept God's will."

A parishioner in one church experienced one disappointment after another. After two deaths in her family she said, "I just must bear my cross."

I said, "Peg, where were you baptized?"
She said, "On my forehead."

**your will**

I said, "Could it be that you were baptized on the wrong end because you seem to be dragging your cross? God's will is always out ahead of us. God's will always has an abundance of his strength for its accomplishment."

Jesus chose the cross; God did not will this for his Son. However, he did will the way Jesus lived and loved up to that cross, and he willed the way he lived and loved and died on the cross. God's will is exciting because the Holy Spirit brings prayer power from its very source.

daily
bread

Our Lord points out the way of wholeness for our temporal needs. The need for the present is sustenance and health—"daily bread"—and not forgetting to be thankful. So thankful, in fact, that those who do pray should seek to share their bread, livelihood, and social concern with the "least of these," as with the Lord.

A recent news article in the *Los Angeles Times* was headed: PIETY SEEN INCREASING CONCERN ON SOCIAL ISSUES. "Religious devotionalism, sometimes scorned by liberal churchmen as a cop-out from life, actually increases concern for social issues, two liberal sociologists have found.

social
concern

"Thomas C. Campbell, associate professor of church and community at Chicago Theological Seminary, and Yoshio Fukugama, professor of religious studies at Pennsylvania State College have authored a new book, *The Fragmented Layman*—a study of 8000 persons. Another study in the Roman Catholic diocese of Trenton was by the Opinion Research Corporation, Princeton, N. J.

"Before making this study, the researchers expected that piety would accompany conservative attitudes on public issues. This was not borne out. Racial attitudes were measured by degrees of social acceptance of blacks and support for their civil rights. At this point the more

38

pious were more liberal than the less devout. "Those indicating a significant pious attitude, by daily prayer and devotional activity, scored substantially higher than others in their willingness to accept minority representatives as neighbors and the support for social justice."*

In terms of the past, every man needs to be free in his conscience from polluted memories —guilt, regret, and self-condemnation. True, we can never be innocent again, but forgiveness can be ours repeatedly. Sin is not like some **forgiveness** bullet that has wounded us which we must carry around and which hurts on rainy days of the soul. It can be removed, we can be healed, so that joyfully we pray, "Forgive us," and we promise to forgive everyone else.

In prayer, we see our chief need for the future—confidence. Our Lord says trust God to lead and to deliver. Although we do not know what the future holds, what joy that we can know him who holds the future in his hands! **guidance** His promise is, "When the Spirit of truth comes, he will guide you into all the truth" (John 16:13).

In Bernard Shaw's play, *St. Joan*, we have this dialogue:

> *Robert:* How do you hear voices?
> *Joan:*  I hear voices telling me what to do. They come from God.
> *Robert:* They come from your imagination.
> *Joan:*  Of course. That's how the messages of God come to us.

We live in a pressure-cooker age. In spite of our arrogance, we need God for our temporal

---

* Used by permission of the *Los Angeles Times*.

requirements, but, equally, we find in him timeless meaning, constant mercy, and future direction. In our pride often we do not want to be
beholden to anyone—not even to God. We recall Peter's saying to Jesus, "You shall never
wash my feet" (John 13:8). This is as unchris-
tian as it is natural, yet immature.

Failing to pray is to act immaturely, as if we
were independent of our heavenly Father and
in no need of the wholeness that his gifts can
bestow. Dr. Alexis Carrel, late fellow of the
American College of Surgeons and Nobel Prize
winner, writes, "Properly understood, prayer is
a mature activity, indispensable to the fullest
development of personality, the ultimate inte-
gration of man's highest faculties.

"Prayer is the frontier where man's need and
God's strength meet. It requires no passport nor
visa. It is the frontier to which we can come in
any state of grace or disgrace."[3]

If our first thought in regard to prayer is,
What would God do for me? the second is,
What can I do for him? It may well surprise
**God** some of us that God needs weak reeds and self-
**needs** centered rebels like ourselves to help accom-
**me** plish his will in the world.

If the late Bishop Fiske is right when he
wrote, "What Jesus was, God is, what Jesus did,
God is always doing," then the Christian God,
as seen in Jesus, is not all-powerful as a dicta-
tor. His omnipotence toward man is that he is
powerful in every situation to love. God is all-
powerful as a lover. In the realm of human nature he has chosen to limit himself to do only
what love will do.

Love is never one-sided or independent; it is
always interdependent. God's need is as acute
as ours. We recall in a certain village it was re-

ported, "He did not do many mighty works there, because of their unbelief" (Matt. 13:58). He only healed a few who knew their real need. He said, "I stand at the door and knock; if any one hears my voice and opens the door, I will come in" (Rev. 3:20). Does he not imply, "If not, I cannot. I will not break it down; but I will not stop loving you. I will not stop knocking on the door of your conscience or of your imagination." He also said, "Ask, and it will be given you; seek, and you will find; knock, and it will be opened to you" (Luke 11:9). Does he not imply, "If you do not ask and seek and knock, I cannot enter to give you my love, my freedom, or my wholeness?"

*love inter-dependent*

Pinioned on the cross by men's blindness and bitterness and hate, he could not reach the crowd as a whole. He was able to reach only two people, an admiring thief and a reflective centurion, but only because they reached for him.

The "come" and "go" in Jesus' commands form a steady tempo, like normal breathing:

"Come" take eat; then, "Go" feed the hungry.
"Come" let me lift your burden; "Go" bear one another's.
"Come" learn of me; "Go" teach.
"Come" lame and blind; "Go" heal.
"Come" be forgiven; "Go" forgive your brother.
"Come" apart with me; "Go" into the world.

*Jesus' "come" and "go"*

In short, you need me, and I need you. St. Paul describes how this worked, years later: "He comforts us in all our troubles, so that we in turn may be able to comfort others in any trouble of theirs and to share with them the consolation we ourselves receive from God" (2 Cor. 1:4, NEB).

John Powell, S.J., writes, "If you give yourself to Him He will immediately put you in the service of others one way or another. Do you really want to volunteer for this life of loving? You can't do it on your own. He must do it in you."

He needs us within the walls of the church, but especially in our home, our school, and on the job, to share with others the new meaning to life that prayer and prayer fellowship with others have brought. He depends on us to be his hands and feet and voice in our generation, to remove injustice and incredibility from our land.

Part of what we mean by prayer power, therefore, is discovered from the standpoint of meeting terrific needs. At any moment of my life I am in need of the mercy, love, and direction of God, or He needs me to channel his grace—this joyful gift—in every human relationship.

The prodigal son, on his way out, had needs. "Father, give me my share of your property." He gave it to him. Sooner or later this son had to answer the prayer in his father's heart, "Come home, son." The son returned. His prayer this time was, "Make me your servant." First, "Give me—help me." Then, "Make me—let me help you."

**give me— make me**

I know scores of men, women, and college students whose lives are now full of power because, at one crucial point, they stopped praying for themselves and prayed, "Lord, I will help you." Prayer is reporting for duty!

One young man, particularly, stands out. He was thirty-five, married, with three children.

Life had come apart for him at home, at work, and in his own self-respect. He said, "What do you think I should do?"

something
God
doesn't
know?

"I don't know."

"But aren't you my rector?"

"Yes."

"What do you think we pay you for?"

"You don't pay me much, and you don't pay me to tell you what to do. If I can leave you and Jesus Christ alone, so that you listen to his Holy Spirit, you will find your answer."

"O.K. Let's have prayer." We knelt together at my prayer desk, and he began, "Dear God, help me . . ."

I said, "Wait a minute, stand up. Why not tell God something he doesn't know? He knows your needs. He has heard you for the last hour."

"Is there anything he does not know?"

"Yes, he does not know how far you will take his help if he gives it to you. Are you willing to say, '*I will help you,* Lord, with my family, in my work, and in all my habits from here on out'?"

"But if I say that, then I will have to turn everything over to him. You see, between the time I left the chair and we got to the prayer desk, I thought of one other thing I hadn't confessed, and I will have to give that over, won't I, if I say 'I'll help you'?" He did just that, and a new day started for him, for his family, and for his friends. *

Why pray? First, we need God. In prayer,

---

* Although I am confident that the person in this story, and other persons whose stories are recounted, would be willing to be known, for in almost all cases they have shared them to the glory of God, I have nevertheless used fictitious names.

"whole"
not
"holy"

we become, not more holy, but more whole.[4] Dr. Carrel said, "The influence of prayer on the human mind and body is as demonstrable as that of secreting glands: a tranquility of bearing, a facial and bodily repose are observed in those whose inner lives are so enriched."[5]

Second, "Every one to whom much is given, of him will much be required" (Luke 12:48). Having become rightly related to God through Jesus Christ in prayer and made whole, we seek to be rightly related to the needs of God in the world and in other lives in order to fulfill our ministry.

Because we often talk of "killing time" or "wasting time," every moment in the life of a Christian is that small part of eternity where we either need God or he needs us. No bit of time is unimportant. There is no moment when we are not praying though we are not always saying our prayers.

St. Theresa of Avila put it this way, "There are three modes of prayer: vocal, silent, and perpetual."[6]

# how to pray

*This chapter was not in the first printing of this book, but is included now because of a letter I received from a Midwest neurologist who began: "You have shown me that I need to pray because, with patients who are dying, I hate them to look into my eyes and to see my dread and hopelessness. But," he continued, "you didn't tell me how to pray . . ."*

*The following is my reply, and I include it in the hope that it will be helpful to other readers as well:*

Dear Doctor ————,

Your letter was good to receive. I have reread it several times and am pleased that here and there my words have struck responsive notes. One thing you said was missing: *How* to pray. Historically there have been two approaches to an intimate rich relationship with God, and all prayer comes within these extremes.

1. One is the monastic appeal with praise, thanksgiving, petition, repentance, and intercession, according to numerous liturgies. Here prayers are addressed to God as Father of Jesus, Creator, and Judge—pouring out our needs and seeking help. Churches with a liturgy— Roman, Anglican, Orthodox, Lutheran—show this influence.

2. At the other extreme is the meditative approach in which the person at prayer seeks to be *acted* upon by God the Holy Spirit. The

Quakers use this—quiet, without set prayers or sacraments, absorbing His love and seeking to be moved by the Spirit.

In the first of these approaches we act toward God. In the second He acts upon us. A balanced prayer life includes both.

I am glad I was taught through the Prayer Book the ancient prayers expressing the needs of the human spirit. Some nights, when sleep is interrupted, I do not stew around. I find that in reciting the Lord's Prayer, the Creed, the Ten Commandments, the Venite, and prayers from the Communion service, my trust is strengthened by trust in these ancient expressions.

In the morning, my most fruitful exercise in bed, sitting or on my knees, is informal: "Good Morning, God" (instead of "Good God, Morning!"). "Thank you, Lord, for this new day. It is yours—what are my marching orders?"

You will note that several times in my book I have suggested the use of paper and pencil. For over fifty years they have been as important to me as Prayer Book, Chalice, or Paten. I list persons whom I will see that day, praying for needs I know they have. I seek ideas and guidance for problems. I would help bring calm to the restless, confused, tense, or fearful around me—not because I am a priest but because I am a man who would be a channel for God's love.

We begin not in agreement with the Christian life but with commitment to Christ. For me in Princeton it took struggle and then commitment. And it is not a "once and for all" thing. It is a daily exercise, because each new day brings not only opportunities for the Good News life but also (in attractive guises) temptations to stop advancing. We seek bread for the *spirit* daily, as well as daily bread for *physical health*.

Your letter in several places shows a hunger for this commitment and its resources:

1. *You say, "I detect a resistance to let go and to accept an unreal and unseen myth."* I too had to wrestle with this, and light came in a college biology lecture, when I thought, "Why isn't the atheist right—or the agnostic?" The professor had drawn on the blackboard the cross-section of an earthworm—something he had seen through a microscope. We were to draw what we saw on our own papers.

Since we had not seen the earthworm ourselves, what the professor drew on the board was to us unreal—a myth. Sitting in that lecture hall with four hundred other students, I imagined three possible attitudes a student in that class might take:

(a) The student—without experimenting—could dismiss the professor's statements as myth, and say "I don't believe that's what he saw." This is the attitude of the atheist.

(b) Another student—also without experimenting—could say, "I don't know if he is right and I will not follow his directions. This is the agnostic's attitude.

(c) The student who is willing to experiment, willing to step out on the professor's hypothesis or conjecture, who commits himself to what he will see for himself, would take a look. That is the path of true science—and of true religious discovery. The student will say, "I'm sorry, professor, but all I see is an indistinct blur!" And the professor's answer will be, "You will find a small nob on the side that will help." So with a twist or two right or left there comes into focus something very real and exciting. And it is no longer only the professor's but the student's also. The student's pencil produces something like the professor's drawing—not complete but, as a start, very real to him.

It came to me that when we adjust—and readjust—our moral, social, and daily actions to Jesus Christ, He leads us to an experience of God. He is "the same today, yesterday, and forever." We are the ones out of focus. We run behind Him when His challenge is too tough; we run ahead of Him when we want to play God.

Some circles (thinking themselves scientific—but actually pseudoscientific) think it sophisticated to be agnostic or atheistic, to spiritually sit on a fence and make no experiments and no commitments. But for me, life is too short to be satisfied with a question mark when an exclamation point is available! Or rather a Cross, which is God's great plus sign for His children. Someone has said "Let go and let God."

2. *You ask "I was brought up Christian, where did I go bad?"* Doctor, you didn't go wrong; you just didn't go far enough. You settled for an arrested spiritual development. There are millions who are retarded like that. I once baptized a man over ninety years of age—a man whose new experience of God made him years younger than some tired old teenagers I have known.

Some time after my decision in college (see Chapter 1) I went home for a vacation. Parties, late hours, fatigue crowded out my morning "quiet time" and Bible reading. I recall becoming morose, overcritical of my parents, and miserable. Happily I stopped to ask why. I read the gospel nearest my birthday. It was the story of Jesus at twelve years of age being forgotten by Mary and Joseph. They had supposed he was with the caravan leaving Jerusalem; when after a day's journey they missed him and returned to the city, they found Him where they had left Him—"about His Father's business."

I realized that Jesus wasn't lost; His parents were. He was about His Father's business but not *with them about it*. If Mary and Joseph couldn't go one day without Him why should I think I could go a month—a week—"supposing." Yet my spiritual biography is marred with one "supposing" after another. Happily, it is also full of the recovering of His companionship again and again. Doctor, you didn't *go bad*. You just didn't go.

3. *You write, "God knows what I want. If He thought I ought to have it, He'd let it be."* You are right if you equate prayer *solely* with petitions, but prayer and prayer power is for more than asking for things. The prime example of the point you make is Jesus' prayer in the garden of Gethsemane the night before the crucifixion. He wanted no part of the suffering, the ridicule, and the agony of the Cross. He prayed that it might pass. This has been called the great unanswered prayer of Jesus. But not so. The Father answered the Son—by giving Him the power of love to see it through (much more important than an escape).

Over the years, I have become more and more conscious of the need *for me to answer His prayer,* the need of bringing my will and plans in line with His, which is maximum use of me as I live among His children who have missed knowing His love.

In the short fifteen minutes between my father's heart attack and his death, I remember kneeling by his bedside with two prayers: "Dear God, give him back" and "Dear God, take him; you know best." When he died I felt that God had released me from possessiveness, rebellion, and hopelessness. I could say "Au revoir" and not "goodbye," except as "goodbye" is the English contraction of "God be with you."

4. *You say, "I have not completely died, because I am involved in life. With each dying person I attend, I pray (ask) for strength to face him with courage, so not to reflect from my eyes my own dread and helplessness."* One cannot give what one does not possess. Your privilege as a physician is to give a patient the best you know—and you do. Your privilege as a human being toward other struggling human beings is to transmit a living faith, deep and resourceful, by your own confidence in God and your joy (not "dread" or "hopelessness.")

I know one physician who said that over the past fifty years he would have gone nuts "if I had to face death without a real faith in a loving God and the resurrection of Jesus." He continued, "I must give my patients more than years to live; I must give them something to live *for.*" He never forced his faith on others; it came through his eyes. When one asks, "How do you get that way?" he shares what he knows to be true.

You asked how to pray. I don't think I answered that—but let's leave it this way:

1. When you are real, and honest, when you

put up no defenses and no sham, how do you talk with your children? How do you talk with your friends? That's the way little children talk to their father. That's the way to pray.

2. When this came clearly to me, then the prayers of the church down through the ages came alive—and do so every Sunday.

3. Between private prayer and public worship—to be in a small praying group enriches points one and two.

You are patient to have read to the end.

Yours in Christ,
J. MOULTON THOMAS

# 5

## some obstacles to prayer

*Man stands upon the poles of Earth,*
*But one thing needed: Second Birth.*
*He marks and streaks the upper air,*
*But is no higher than his prayer.*
NANCY TIER

A CHILD WAS ASKED, "How do you keep up with your father? He's tall, and he takes such big steps."

"Oh, that's easy," said the child. "I reach up as high as I can go, and he comes down all the rest of the way, and then we go along a kitin'."

If "Jesus Christ is the same yesterday, today, and forever," if "the Father is more ready to hear than we to pray," and if his Holy Spirit is more eager to guide than we to follow, then any failure in prayer lies not with him. The failure must be in our reach. Somewhere we are muscle-bound. Here are four reasons why our reach may be limited:

inadequate
time

First, I may give inadequate time to prayer and to the Bible. Time with the Bible is essential if I would go to the original documents of God's revelation in history, if I would join Jesus' first disciples in listening to his words, and to the later letters of his friends, telling of his con-

tinuing companionship. They are addressed to
me as well. So often the Bible is the inspired
book that is suitable to the *needs of my neighbor*. I find, in reading Scripture, that things do
not happen so much in Palestine as they happen in me.*

St. Paul urges young Timothy to read the
Scriptures. "Continue in what you have learned
and have firmly believed, knowing from whom
you learned it and how from childhood you
have been acquainted with the sacred writings
which are able to instruct you for salvation
through faith in Christ Jesus. All scripture is
inspired by God and profitable for teaching, for
reproof, for correction, and for training in right-
eousness, that the man of God may be complete, equipped for every good work" (2 Tim.
3:14–17).

Some time each day I will take apart for my
prayer life whether I feel like it or not. Archbishop Whealon, the Roman Catholic Archbishop of Hartford, put it this way, "The person who prays only when he feels like it doesn't
pray very much."

Dag Hammarskjøld wrote: "God does not die
on the day we cease to believe in a personal
deity, but we die on the day when our lives
cease to be illuminated by the steady radiance
of wonder, the Source of which is beyond all
reason."[1]

*to
wonder*

Bishop Bardsley of Coventry suggested, "Be
still enough to be able to hear the clock tick,
and to wonder. What does God think of me?
In what direction is my life going? What do I

---

* I recommend the excellent material of the Bible
Reading Fellowship in Winter Park, Florida.

give to people: false faces and a phony sincerity, or deep concern, arising from a contemplative personality?"

Martin Luther reportedly said, "I will be so busy today, I must take two hours for prayer instead of one."

**to**
**listen**
To spend some time each day in quiet and to listen is not only good for the soul but for mind and body as well. In the play *Generation* the daughter says, "Dad, it looks like the race you are running is running you."

The bishop of Birmingham, England, wrote, "Clergy today have lost an inner beauty by allowing themselves to be pressured."

A physician said that the average businessman is not living out his normal life expectancy. Insecurity and nervous distress are wreaking havoc. He is dying far too young.

"For an age that believes in incessant action," William Barclay writes in *The Promise of the Spirit*, "silent waiting is an unpalatable prescription. For a man whose every waking moment is occupied—who even steals time for work from the hours of sleep—there may be necessary a complete reorganization of life, if he is to find time for this silent waiting on the Spirit. It is hard to find time for that apparent 'doing nothing' which means everything."[2]

In Leonard Bernstein's *Mass*, performed by Yale students on TV April 23, 1975, the priest-figure is tormented by his memories, his doubts, and other agonies. The wild crisscross running of actors and the cacophony of choir and orchestra are suddenly silenced when in distress he cries out, "Let us pray!" How eloquent and commanding that silence.

We must go into the closet, be quiet, and relax. In silence, God speaks, not to the ear, but from his loving heart to ours. "He who made the heart does he not love? He who made the eyes, does he not see? He who made the ear does he not hear? He who made the lips, does he not speak?" Like invisible air waves, in our room all the time, which require that we tune in and listen, God's love always surrounds us. The assurance of his presence for our correction or direction is available.

Mother Teresa of Calcutta speaks with poetic beauty about silence:

> We need to find God. He cannot be found in noise and restlessness. God is the friend of silence: trees, flowers, grass. See the stars and how they move in silence. The more we receive in silent prayer, the more we can give in our active life. The essential thing is not what *we* say but what God says to us and then through us. Words that do not give the light of Christ increase the darkness.[3]

*be still and know*

"If we are to receive 'saving health' from the Lord of Life we must compose our souls, as we do when we stand before any great art, or listen to any great music. We simply open up to Beethoven, or Shakespeare, or Michelangelo —or Christ. Another word for that receptivity is humility."[4]

John Powell in *He Touched Me* says, "So He comes to me in the listening, receptive moments of prayer, and he transfuses His power into me; he rekindles my desires to be His man; to be a public utility, a town pump for the kingdom of God—just as His son was during His life among us."

In these periods of quiet and listening, we are

able to see our lives with a little more detachment. Here we can check our short-term ambitions and aims against what we desire to be the overall direction of our lives.

escapism?

Activists might call this escapism. We have to ask, Was Jesus an escapist? He spent forty days apart in the wilderness at the beginning of his ministry, wrestling with decisions and temptations (not between good and evil so much as between the best and the mediocre). He spent all night in prayer before choosing his twelve apostles, and it was recorded, "In the morning, a great while before day, he rose and went out to a lonely place, and there he prayed" (Mark 1:35). His prayer life must have been extremely creative to lead the disciples to say, "Lord, teach us to pray." He ended his ministry all night apart in prayer in Gethsemane, and three of the last seven words men heard were prayers.

If Jesus needed to take time apart from his activities, how dare I, signed with his cross, take no time, or give a passing nod, "a lick and a promise"? Yes, I can work for the kingdom of God. I can *say* my prayers. I can join the congregation in prayer, but it will not be praying unless I listen also. Then I discover the psalmist's secret, "Be still and know."

A second obstacle to a vital experience of prayer could be that we put someone before Jesus Christ in our living and loving. This is known as an idol.* It could be husband, wife, or child.

On a train between Baltimore and Washington, a young woman sat next to me. She ap-

---

* Romans 1:22–25.

peared very fearful. She told me she had had to leave her five-year-old daughter at Johns Hopkins Hospital. The child meant "everything to her." Before arriving in Washington, we had prayer together, in which she put her daughter in God's care. "I give her back to you, Lord, who gave her to us. Forgive me for putting her first." **idols**

A week later her letter came from South Carolina: "When my husband met me at the station, he was surprised at my calm, and said that Betty must surely be out of danger. 'When is she coming home?' 'I don't know, but I do know one thing: when I admitted my possessiveness, my fear left, and I felt God's arms beneath all three of us.'"

Another idol is described by Studdert-Kennedy in four lines called "Temptation":

Pray! Have I prayed! When I'm worn with all
my praying!

When I've bored the blessed angels with my
battery of prayer.

It's the proper thing to say—but it's only
saying, saying,

And I cannot get to Jesus for the glory of
her hair.[5]

A third block to prayer is self-pity. It is a clergy obstacle, believe me. We are not always appreciated at home or by our people. When problems seem too great, we may hear of a vacant parish, and our imagination takes over. How would I look in that other pulpit? **self-pity**

Often self-pity asks, Why did this happen to me? In the eternal scheme of things we may

why?
nol
where?

never know. Sometimes the reasons we give may or may not be true. But it is almost certain that those who seek God's next—and usually exciting—steps, who wrestle in prayer to find his will, do not have time to ask why.

The true answer to why is another question, Where? Once in a storm on the sea of Galilee, Jesus was awakened by his fearful friends as he slept in the stern. They said, "Why did this happen to us? Don't you care if we drown?"

He did not answer the why. He "rebuked" the winds, then rebuked the disciples. "Where is your faith? Where is your trust that, when I am in your boat, there is no need for fear?"

Self-pity asks "Why?" Jesus asks "Where?"

After a radio service, one Lent, I had a call from a listener. "I am most unhappy—my husband has changed his job, we have moved, I had to leave behind my beautiful garden. Now I am in a small apartment. The neighbors are unfriendly, and the minister hasn't called. What ought I do?"

"I suggest that you confess your sins."

Being a good Episcopalian, she said, "What sins?"

"My friend, self-pity has been coming through this telephone wire for five minutes. I am sitting here in three inches of it."

"But I can't get to church, I have high blood pressure."

"You know, God gave us a radio so you could hear me, and he gave us a telephone so I could hear you."

After a moment of silence she prayed, "Dear God, forgive me for putting myself first."

I used the prayer of absolution, and she promised to phone next week.

"Hello," she said, "this is me." (I never did

know her name.) "This has been a great week. The neighbors have been most friendly. There's lots to do in the apartment, and the doctor has just left—my blood pressure is down twenty points. Aren't you surprised?"

"Not at all—I'd have been surprised if you had been your same old unhappy self."

A fourth obstacle to prayer's reality is an overconscientious effort on our part. Our Lord said, "The Gentiles think that they will be heard from their much praying." It is counterproductive to pray too hard, that is, with "faithless fears and worldly anxiety."

An older couple with their granddaughter drove over an embankment and into a canal. When I called at the hospital, the husband was bandaged from head to foot. The child, unharmed, was asleep. The wife, with two broken ribs, was in great pain and quite fearful. For the past three hours sedatives had had no relaxing effect.

"I am praying hard"

I introduced myself and offered to be of assistance. Then I asked, "What are you doing to help yourself?"

"I am praying very hard," she replied.

I am sure that my reply was not expected. "I think you are praying too hard. You give me the impression of someone standing high on a stepladder trying to beat in the gates of heaven. God isn't way up there. He is like the ladder; turn around and sit down. Think of this bed as God's arms. While I have a prayer, I will put my hand under your shoulder, and I want to feel your muscles relax." It was a short prayer, and she was asleep before I finished.

turn around, sit down

Two weeks later, after they had arrived home in Cincinnati, she wrote, "I have just come back from the cemetery. Mr. Joyce developed an embolism and died quite suddenly; but I do want to tell you that when I saw his body being lowered into the ground, I remembered my discovery of the kind of prayer that really trusts. So I put him in our Lord's hands, and I know now the victory that overcomes death itself."

Sam Shoemaker told of a young bride who was terrified at the thought of having to cook three meals a day for fifty years. "She was so relieved when she discovered how much the fire did." Are we praying too hard?

# more obstacles—
# then breakthrough

*"By thee I can crush a troop; and by my
God I can leap over a wall"* (Ps. 18:29).

A FIFTH OBSTACLE to the reality of prayer is
holding resentment or bitterness toward another
person. Our Lord said, "When you pray, forgive."

A college professor told me he was leaving
to accept an offer from a Western university—
with higher salary and increase in rank (from
assistant to associate professor). I congratu-
lated him but asked, "Why?"

resentment

"I should have been promoted here. The men
who came when I did have been raised. So this
offer is much more interesting."

"You seem a little bitter against the dean."

"I am."

He had been a member of a weekly prayer
group consisting of several faculty members,
students, and businessmen.

"Have you prayed about it?"

"No."

"Why not?"

"Because God might tell me to stay."

"I don't know about that, but this is the time

to surrender your bitterness wherever you teach."

"I suppose that's really why I came to see you."

When he submitted in prayer, he found God's forgiveness, and the dean looked so much better.

a
professor

First, he wired the university that he had changed his mind. Second, like Moses in Egypt, he discovered that the ground on which he had hated to stand was now, with God, holy ground. Two months later, at a weekday chapel service, his topic was "A Second Language for Everyone—Prayer."

The word fraternity means brotherhood, but it can mean tribal hostility toward members of other fraternities. Such was the battle between two on the Trinity College Campus. It had become so acrid that material damage to the property of each was a daily occurrence. The dean threatened both groups with social probation.

That year—and for eight years—a small group of six or ten students met in my study for prayer on Thursday nights from ten until eleven-thirty. This was to sharpen our faith and to keep us spiritually concerned about student problems and campus situations. It was not an announced activity. Each year it was a great help to me, as chaplain, to have the "Christian underground."

In this group there happened to be one member of each fraternity. For two Thursday evenings we made these hostilities a matter for intercessory prayer and for guidance. After one of our periods of quiet listening, there came to us clearly three goals or steps to action. I have forgotten just what they were, but each of the fraternity members felt that if agreement could be reached on these points, good relations could be restored.

When they presented them to their own fraternities (not telling where they originated), each brought these basics for arbitration. When, in a meeting of the two fraternities, each offered the same three, they were dumbfounded at the coincidence.

Not until published here has the truth been known about the "coincidence," the result of a small group with prayer power.

Several years ago a young atomic scientist became a member of the church. His was a rich experience of the Holy Spirit and of God's freedom from many burdens. Prayer became real to him in private, at Holy Communion, and in a small fellowship of businessmen.

One day he said, "I don't seem to be able to pray."

"Just how long has this been going on?"

He said, "For two weeks."

an
atomic
scientist

So we talked for a while. Then it came out that the chief of the atomic lab at the university had, in a Rotary Club talk, claimed the discovery of something that was Bob's. This was resented by some other colleagues, and Bob became bitter himself.

We had some quiet, and then in prayer he asked God's forgiveness.

Next Sunday at early service, he had his former joy again, and he told me why. "I went to Bill the next day and apologized for holding this resentment. Bill said, 'You don't have to ask my forgiveness, I am the stinker in this thing.' 'Yes, I know you are, but I need to clean up my part as well.' Bill said, 'How do you happen to look at it this way?' 'Because three months ago when I was confirmed I learned to pray, and I learned how to be a whole person. But, so long as I was bitter against you, I couldn't reach my Lord.'"

He told me two results of this new relationship with Bill. First, there was a new unity and new spirit in the lab. Second, Bill, who for two years had been a lapsed Roman Catholic, was back at his mass this very day.

Forgiveness and love purify the spiritual air and the human environment, and the world is in far greater crisis from this moral pollution than from drying lakes and poisoned rivers. We so often think, "What can I do for ecology?"

When I forgive and find love for one person, I have begun where I am and I become part of the cure instead of being part of the disease.

racial violence and love

In 1968 two students were killed in confrontation with the state troopers in Orangeburg, S.C. Four days later at a conference on Prayer Power we heard one woman, a retired black professor of chemistry, say "When I first heard of the shootings, I was afraid and angry and full of hate. My best friend was the mother of one of those boys. I wanted to go to her, but first I had to get on my knees. I asked God to forgive that trooper that I had feared and hated. Then only could I take life and love with me."

guilt

A sixth block to prayer and prayer power is guilt. Seneca wrote, "the mind is never right until it is at peace with itself." A psychiatrist said that the condition of our souls affects the condition of our minds and bodies. When we have an unclear conscience, the heart pounds. We find concentration at work or at studies difficult, and at night we are restless and wakeful. Fine men would not crack up if their souls were free of guilt.

There are four things we can do about this inner contradiction and disease. First, we can persuade ourselves that a guilty conscience is now out of date.[1] The reasoning goes something like this: to be guilty is just a hangover from Victorian morality. There is no absolute truth, no divine law, no judge or judgment, now or hereafter. Simply act according to one's self-centered changeable standards, that is, according to the "devices and desires of our own hearts." Anything that produces a conviction of sin is psychologically bad and in bad taste. Don't we have mental health clinics and self-awareness programs that can exorcise the demons of negative feelings and provide instant tranquillity? And don't we have psychiatrists? Religion, therefore, has done an infinite amount of harm and it is ridiculous to think of one man carrying the weight for all mankind. (See 1 John 8–9.) In *Bad Habits*, a play by Terrance McNally, the chief therapist offers cures through capitulation to one's vices.

It may do us good to remember that the laws of nature are not broken, though they may be disobeyed. I climb a steeple to test the law of gravity. I say that I am going to break it. So I jump. I do not break the law. I am likely to break something else. There are laws of human nature that cannot be broken: the Ten Commandments, and our Lord's summary of the law. "God didn't hand down 'The Ten Suggestions.'"[2] I may disobey, but I cannot break them. I will break something else. It may be another's trust. It could be another's heart. It will be my own self-respect. In short, I break

*how to cope*

*sin is out of date*

*unbreakable laws?*

65

myself. I dim my vision of truth, of purity, and of God's reality. Dr. Francis Braceland, when he was professor of psychiatry at Yale, said, "One reason for the rise in the need for psychiatrists for high school and college girls, can be traced to the so-called 'new morality.'"

Writing in the *Journal of the American Medical Association*, Dr. Robert Collins of Syracuse, N.Y., says, "'New Morality' is a fad—it ignores history. It denies the physical and mental composition of human beings. It is intolerant; it is exploitive. It is oriented toward intercourse, not love. The unity and community that couples seek cannot be accomplished at the pelvic level."

"Life is more than sexual combustibility."[3]

Dr. Collins continues, "Sex 'for kicks' isn't real—it resembles the animal coitus and ignores a basic characteristic of humans—the need for love and the need to be loved; the need to care and the need to be cared for. Sexuality and its physical expression must be part of the whole personality. To develop these is a major life's goal, and needs a climate of patience, understanding, and most important, time."[4]

Quite in contrast to "Sin is Out of Date" is the message of Alexander Solzhenitsyn of whom William Shannon (*New York Times,* July 16, 1975) writes, "He is a uniquely Russian prophet who became an exile in the wilderness of the west. He speaks of sin, shame and redemption, concepts which our neo-pagan society with its secularized atmosphere and deeply corrupt popular culture can barely comprehend."

Well, that is one way to treat guilt: to proclaim that we are liberated by the permissive revolution.

Michel Quoist writes: "The world is filled

with talk of revolution—but there is only one true revolution—that which will make all things new, beginning with the heart of man in the depth of himself which man himself cannot reach—and then by extending to the least and the greatest of our economic, political and social structure until it affects the whole universe."[5]

**true revolution**

Dr. Benjamin Spock speculates that experts like himself may have encouraged a generation of parents to evade their own responsibilities.[6] He laments the reputation he has acquired for encouraging parental permissiveness—*20 million copies too late.*

**second thoughts**

New York psychiatrist, Richard Robertiello, has rethought his once permissive policies on child rearing. The children of permissiveness are now his psychiatric patients, "loveable, but they can't hang on to anything. They can't master anything."[7]

I don't think I am easily shocked, but I was a little speechless with the remark of the chaplain of a prominent seminary. We were at a luncheon table with six students. The subject was prayer and praying together. One student said: "We study monastic rules of prayer and the theology of prayer. We attend chapel, but naturally and informally, we do not pray."

The chaplain added, "No, we do not tell our students that they ought to pray. It might make them feel guilty if we told them to and they didn't."[8]

Of a devoted parishioner, Sam Shoemaker said, "She has every virtue except a sense of sin."

How can we avoid seeing in governmental, political, and international immorality the prior corruption of personal morality? Break the commandments, we cannot; by indifference and neglect, we break ourselves, our homes, and our country.

Can it be that the situation ethics of the '50s and '60s have come home to haunt us?

Fred Pope, cartoonist for *The Living Church,* aptly puts it this way:[9]

*We do not speak of "sin and forgiveness" today, but rather of our total adjustment that has had some negative learning experiences which might well be made viable through new and creative adjustments . . . or so it seems to me.*

The son of a college professor of adjustment psychology brought home from school a failing report.

"This is a great disappointment," said the professor, "please explain."

"Well, dad, you see I've decided to adjust to lower grades."

W. Irving Harris, first editor of *Faith at Work* magazine, writes in his forthcoming book:

just
adjust

Under the spell of a certain kind of psychiatrist, many people today seem to dread the state of "feeling guilty."

All I can say is that the nearer I moved toward Jesus, I moved toward a new release of freedom, for the shame was not building up to remorse, but moving me toward repentance—the willingness to say "I'm sorry." Like the prodigal, I needed forgiveness. I slipped to my knees by the side of my bed, and cried for a new chance.

**freedom**

An amazing thing happened. Into my heart flooded a sense of relief. I knew, beyond all question, God was within me, and the Holy Spirit was a veritable breath which invaded my mind and heart, and claimed me for Himself.[10]

George Adam Smith wrote, "The forgiveness of God is the foundation of every bridge from a hopeless past to a courageous present."[11]

If the first treatment of guilt is to deny it, the second is to try to forget it with the help of alcohol, drugs, sleeping pills, and/or finally suicide. The only trouble is, except for the last, we have to "come to."

**"forget it"**

A third way of dealing with guilt is to attempt to cover our moral failures with good works. I am reminded of the boy scout who went for an overnight hike. He put his sleeping bag on the ground and crawled in, but he felt a rock underneath. He walked three miles back to town and carried out a mattress. He couldn't sleep; so he went back two more times, and soon he had three mattresses beneath the sleeping bag. He still couldn't get to sleep. He had to get out the rock.

A quotation from Homer shows approaching

God via good works is as old as the Trojan War.
Chryses prays to Apollo:

Hear me, Lord of the silver bow,
If I have ever roofed over a temple pleasing to you,
If I have burned in your honor, fatted thighs of
    bulls or goats,
Then accomplish this my prayer.[12]

the
cover-up

No human effort for good can cover any sin
in our memory, nor can any human effort for
good earn a clean heart. If we could be as
perfect as Jesus Christ for the next thirty years,
we would not cover up one failure of the past.
It would take the next thirty years to accomplish
such perfection (if we could do it) with no
personal credit left over to apply to our past.
Nor is there a treasury of merit available from
other people, from Jesus' friends, from the
saints, or from Jesus' mother. There are only
"the merits and mediation of our Lord and
Savior, Jesus Christ," his offered extra love and
forgiveness after confession. This is called his
grace, freely given from his cross and completely unearned.

An active church member died and wanted
to get to heaven. He was met at the gate by
St. Peter and told that he would have to have
one hundred credits. He said, "All right, I have
been an elder for twenty-five years." He was
told this was good for one credit. "One credit!!!
You don't know what I had to go through with
the ministers that we had. They were awful."

"One credit."

"I also was on the national church board."

"One credit."

"One credit!!! For all that? But I did help

70

in the community, and I gave rather liberally to the church."

"One credit. Can you think of anything else?"

"No, I can't. If I get in, I suppose it will be by the grace of God."

"That's fine," said St. Peter, "come right on in. That's always worth ninety-seven points."

The cross is God's great plus sign in history because it is the place where his grace was first offered. And yet, conscientious clergy and laity persist in trying to cover up failures, hoping to earn the favor of God by good works, and thereby missing prayer power.

A fourth approach to guilt is to decide to be burdened with our failures. *Remorse* is the name for this hopelessness. The French have a word for it, *remodre*, which means literally "bite myself again and again." Self-condemnation fools us into a false humility. It sounds humble to say, "How can God forgive me when I can't even forgive myself?" Actually, this is pride in its most deceptive costume. It is saying, "Lord, I will not let go of my burden. I don't believe you are strong enough to carry it; so I must continue to play God in my own life." At Holy Communion when I come to receive his life and to offer in my hands, my sins, to exchange my sins for his grace, I too often take him *and* my self-condemnation back to the pew and back home. This lets him in only part way because he is still in competition with the other idols. This is not Christian faith because it is not freedom.

Prayer power is realized only when we dump everything over the rail and leave it all there. Happily, in an increasing number of parishes, on either side of the altar is a growing pile of

*[margin note:* self-condemnatio*]*

*[margin note:* breakthrough*]*

garbage-guilt surrendered by human spirits to Jesus Christ *for keeps*. One added value of a free-standing altar is that there is more space now in the sanctuary for our burdens! The result is free-standing Christians in homes, at work, on college campuses, singing with the Good News of God's grace. It is too good to be true, but it is true. Without Jesus Christ, guilt is unhealthy, to be avoided, covered by good works or remorse. With Jesus Christ, guilt is most healthy because in him the Father has more love and forgiveness than I can possibly need to blot it out.

"come
to
me"

Legend tells that after his death the penitent thief came in great confidence to the Father for judgment. God said, "How do you come so happily, considering your evil ways upon the earth?"

The thief replied, "Sir, I was with your Son on another cross this afternoon. He told me to charge everything to his account, and I believed him."[13]

# transition

So far we have briefly presented some basic elements of our faith.

First, *the gospel:* Jesus himself. *Theology:* where God is our intellectual problem. *Religion:* where we are God's problem.

Then we considered the *purpose of prayer:* to be with God because we need him and he needs us.

In the third place, we suggested some *obstacles* that may not keep us from saying our prayers, but do short-circuit relationships with God and our neighbors.

In all these we are describing one's personal faith, one's personal prayer life. That is all well and good because personal prayer life both precedes and accompanies small fellowships of prayer which we will now look at under these topics:

- Prayer Power for Families
- Prayer Power for the Clergy
- Prayer Power for the Church.

Here is a word of warning. There is real danger that a group may become ingrown and "holier than thou." Such unattractive pietistic groups are called, by Bishop Bardsley, "holy huddles." Beware.

# 7

# prayer power for families—
# the initial cost

*"Woman, behold, your son! . . . Behold,
your mother!" (John 19:26–27).*

AFTER THREE HOURS or more on the cross, after
broadcasting forgiveness for Pilate, Herod, Judas,
the soldiers, and the fickle mob, and after prom-
ising a thief paradise with himself, Jesus comforts his mother and his best friend, entrusting
them to each other. "Woman, behold, your son.
Son, your mother." This entreaty was more than
a considerate gesture. On Calvary, the Son of
God laid new foundations for all personal relationships and for every Christian home.

Calvary's
blueprint

A long time ago a country doctor said to me,
"Son, there are three sides to every argument:
my side, your side, and the right side." This
came back to me when I wanted a design for
prayer power in Christian homes. I have my
needs and hopes, you have yours; but together
in seeking God's will is our unity, peace, and
love. Saint-Exupéry wrote, "Love does not consist in gazing at each other, but in looking
together in the same direction."

This triangular relationship, begun on Calvary, was to be the pattern for any Mary and

any John and any Tom, Dick, or Harriet—for Christian friends, for those engaged, for husband and wife, and between the generations. The closer we come to Jesus Christ in prayer together, the closer we find ourselves to one another in understanding, honesty, and freedom.

Every friendship is based on a third common interest. Therefore every relationship is really triangular (see the diagram, page 130). If we drop the interest, we are likely to drift apart. In that case our figure shifts from a triangle to railroad tracks. In some families we parallel each other, not clashing, but just keeping our distance, and like an old tennis ball, the early romance loses its bounce.

On Calvary, Jesus established a new design for human relations in which men and women make him the object of their friendship and love as he calls them into the divine-human fellowship. The movement is not only from the base angles to the apex (which we can never reach in this life) but is primarily from the cross to us. We realize that we have not so much chosen him as he has chosen us because he loves us, he needs us, and will supply us with prayer power as we seek his will.

"I have chosen you"

In Christian marriage we build our new home "through Jesus Christ Our Lord." We love because he first (last and always) loves us.

Jesus said that in marriage two become one flesh. Two do not really become one in civil marriage, in nonmarriage union, or even in a marriage performed in church. In those, the two are still two. The fulfillment of one-flesh union is possible only when both husband and wife are also in triangular union with God.

"And I, when I am lifted up from the earth, will draw all men to myself" (John 12:32).

76

There was another workable triangle on the first Good Friday. With Jesus as their common interest, Pilate and Herod became friends after a long-standing feud.

In light of the home situation which Jesus designed and inspired on Calvary, let us look at (1) the so-called generation gap and (2) the basis for a Christian engagement.

Among graffiti on a wall was this comment on parental problems with offspring: "Avenge yourself! Live long enough to be a problem to your children!" Sometimes we don't have to live very long to be just that. Neither do they. Every generation has experienced the relationship problem. More recently, we have known it as the *generation gap*.

Let's call the generation gap by another name—the *regeneration gap*. This puts the problem where it belongs, that is, in the realm of rebellious human nature. Love produces harmony; less than love is conflict.

Regeneration gap means that the serious conflicts among members of a family (or of society) exist because God's love is not realized sufficiently in individual lives. Paul Tournier, Swiss physician-evangelist, writes, "Members of the same generation are divided. The fracture is not between spouses and children but within each of us."[1]

In one city a physician and his wife had a son, Bill, in high school, and a married daughter. A chasm existed between husband and wife. "We had tripped on our lines of communication somewhere." There were also spaces between the son and the parents.

When their son learned that a new discovery of Christ had brought his parents together, and when he saw a new love between them, he

*regeneration gap*

77

hungered to be part of the emerging new home. One evening at a church youth meeting an experience of praying out loud with his peers showed him the way to ask his parents to let him in on their experience. "When they knew I had found Christ, they said that for a month their prayer was that sister and I would join them."

Bill said, "That night we were honest about ourselves, our hurts and resentments, and prayed together. We had had our problems—mostly stemming from the younger generation—but now in prayer we see each other in a new light of understanding."

In another family in the same church a businessman and his wife didn't think they had spiritual needs. "I was a self-satisfied senior warden with, I believed, everything under control. John saw through all that and made the first move. We think, usually, of parents leading children, but in our house it's the other way around."

John came home from the youth meeting with Bill and said, "Dad, in praying with my high-school friends we have found a secret that makes us more honest and not ashamed to say we need Jesus in everything—and this includes our home."

Father and mother felt this was fine for John! "But mother, you and dad are sitting on the edge of a swimming pool. You've got to jump in to know what I'm talking about."

"We began that night," the father said. "There were many places I needed help, and our new prayer life together has brought us rich companionship and understanding. A serious situation later arose, but in prayer—and

78

guided by God's Spirit—the way through was discovered."

Those were high-school seniors. Grant, a college junior, says, "When I started my first year of college, I commuted from home, living with my parents. Our family atmosphere at that time was far from desirable, as my parents were having serious marital problems.

college age

"Having my own car, my first steady girl, plus being a member of the fire department, I was spending more and more time away from home. This upset my parents and caused much friction between us. Then problems set in with my girl. My marks started slipping too because I was frustrated most of the time. It seemed my whole world was falling apart. I had no one to turn to and no where to go. I had practically given up.

"Then, for some reason, in our home, things started to take a turn for the better. At the time I did not know what it was. I could see my mother was smiling again. My father, whose once-a-year trip to the church had been for the pancake supper, went to each of the Lenten prayer groups. Their attitude toward me had really changed; they seemed to be trying to understand my feelings and wants. How could this be? New life was in our house because mother and father had discovered, in individual surrender to Jesus Christ, a rich relationship with the other. Resource came in their praying together. Their joy was so real.

"If they needed a change, so did I. On the way home from college one day, I couldn't go by our church. I had to go in. There, kneeling, I thanked God for our new home. More than that I needed his forgiveness—and prayed that he would include me in our family fellowship. I knew as I got up, not only the love of God making me whole, but his assurance of direction in the future—I no longer felt lost or alone.

"Gone is the generation gap! We are honestly and openly communicating with a warmth that chases away the kind of conflicts we used to know.

"A few times since this experience, I felt I was losing him, and I was miserable. Then I thought back to the time when I found him in prayer and how great it was, and I told the Lord I wanted to be his again."

**regeneration victory**

Generation gap? Look first for his regeneration victory and Christ's prayer power!

With two out of five American marriages ending in divorce (60 percent of them with children under eighteen), there is no telling how many are cracked like window glass but not shattered enough to fall apart.

A loving, creative Christian home presupposes the rich faith underlying a Christian marriage. Christian engagement presupposes the experience of God's love and his will on the part of two twice-born friends. Admittedly that is some presupposition!

We do know where this Christian nurture is true. Premarital spiritual counseling is one of the great privileges of the ministry. Christian nurture is extended in the process of doing one's best to develop, by beginning with two Christians, a Christian home that will have its creative impact upon the community.

**a Christian engagement**

One couple from Boston met with me in Hartford. Our first meeting went well. The second, a month later, was a disaster. We were talking about relations with their future in-laws. Great hostility was evident toward his mother.

Bert's father had died when he was two, and his mother had become so possessive that she resented every girl he dated.

Bert was so bitter that when engaged to Susan he moved from Pittsburgh and took a job in Boston.

I talked of forgiveness. Not a chance. I mentioned, "Forgive us as we forgive." No response. I quoted, "Father, forgive" Pilate, Herod, Judas, the soldiers.

"I don't believe that Jesus would forgive her!"

I could only tell them that hatred would be like deadly poison if carried into their new home. They said they could cope with that. Then I had to say that in all honesty I could not perform the wedding ceremony. When I would have to say, "Whom God hath joined together," I would be lying.

With real sadness on my part, they chose to leave. This happened on Palm Sunday night; the wedding was scheduled for June.

The following Wednesday I received this note in the mail:

> We left your house upset and angry at you. For an hour we traveled in silence. Then at almost the same moment we said something like, "How blind we have been. How wrong. How far away we have pushed God." We stopped the car, pulled to the side of the road, and had prayer together, asking his forgiveness. We felt a new warmth toward mother and new depth of love for each other. Will you marry us in June?

*evidence of the resurrection*

I replied:

> With the greatest joy—and one other thing. Your discovery is the best Easter

greeting I could imagine. It's contemporary evidence that Christ—who was dead in you—is now alive. Happy Easter. I'll see you in June.

Their Christian engagement now could lead to Christian marriage and the possibility of a Christian home.

On Calvary, Jesus Christ gave his design for, laid his foundations for, and made the costly down payment for a new home situation for the whole human family.

# prayer power for families— upkeep and outreach

*"It is not marriage that fails. People fail.
All that marriage does is to show people up."*
Harry Emerson Fosdick

HARTFORD, CONNECTICUT, is the insurance capital of the United States. A number of years ago, on a train from Hartford to Baltimore, I sat next to a keen young man who seemed very eager to talk. It was soon apparent that for the past ten days he had been attending a special training school at one of the Hartford insurance companies. He knew all the new policies, and from the glint in his eye he was quite sure that insurance would save the world. Not wearing a clerical collar that day, I listened and asked numerous questions about the new policies and new approaches of his company. This went on far past New Haven, and then he said, "And what do you do?"

I said, "I am in insurance also."

Well, this must have been a shock. I am sure he wondered what secrets he had divulged to a competitor. But, collecting himself, he said, "What kind of insurance do you carry?"

I said, "Numerous kinds. Three especially. First is life because I represent the Life Assur-

marriage insurance

ance Society of the World. Second is fire insurance. Actually we carry 'fire prevention' insurance. Third, and here is the real bargain, we have marriage insurance. We guarantee happy homes."

"Where is your home office?"

"Heaven," I said.

"Then you're a Christian minister?"

"Yes, I am."

I said marriage insurance is not farfetched. Two things are important in any insurance transaction. First, the prospective buyer should read the policy, especially the small print. Second, he must keep up his premiums or the policy will lapse.

The marriage insurance policy (or the sacrament of holy matrimony) contains those two essentials. First, there is the small print, the symbol that is used throughout this service. It **the** describes the secret of all Christian relation-**small** ships. The words and actions are in the shape **print** of a triangle where man and woman, or two sons, or two brothers, or father and son are at the base angles, and Jesus Christ on his cross is at the apex, signifying that the closer they come to him, the closer they come to each other. Furthermore, for Christians, this arrangement symbolizes that two people put the love of Jesus Christ before their love for each other. With his love, they need never run out of love, or patience, one for the other.

This eternal triangle is, first of all, in the exhortation. "We have come together in the presence of *God* to witness and proclaim the joining together of *this man* and *woman* in marriage."[1] It is seen also in the vows: "Will you have this man or woman to live in holy marriage?" "I will," but not in my own strength.

"I will by God's help!" We act this out when the minister asks, "Who gives this woman to be married to this man?" The father says, "I do," but he doesn't give the bride to the groom; he gives the bride to the minister representing Jesus Christ, and the groom receives his bride from God at the hands of his minister.

the eternal triangle

Now we come to the upkeep—our premiums, daily prayer together, at times out loud. As soon as the vow is taken to be loyal one to the other, we hear, "I pronounce that you are husband and wife" and "those whom God has joined together, let no man put asunder."

the premiums

The two are now Mr. and Mrs. Next the couple and all others present join in reciting the Lord's (family) Prayer. The premium we pay for life assurance in the home is a prayer life that continues day after day.

During prayer power weekends of the Anglican Fellowship of Prayer, we have had special sessions for couples. After presenting our insurance pitch, usually two or three couples tell very simply the difference honest prayer has made in their relationship with each other and with their children. Almost all have said that it wasn't easy at first. Church worship together was the closest they had come to praying.

In the presence of forty couples, a husband said: "Prayer is not a thing totally different for my wife and me, but it is something that we have always practiced separately and in private. I think it is a great shame for people who are intimate in every other way not to share the most important part of them, namely, their relationship with God. Although prayer is sacred, it need not be a secret.

sacred but not secret

"After last Saturday's session, we went back to our room and got started. Together we have 'broken the sound barrier' of prayer, and we know the peace of God in our marriage as never before."

A lawyer and his wife were like many in the social whirl. They had two teen-age children. The wife related: "Our family had all it needed and more. We were knee-deep in activities at church, boy scouts, PTA, Community Chest, and so on. We were doing good but not feeling good about it. We knew something was wrong because our lives lacked meaning. We had inherited Christian ideals but didn't really believe they would work because they had been a pushover when put to economic or social tests.

*doing good but not feeling good*

"Our social life made us ask, Is this what life is all about? My false face kept cracking every time I tried to put on a smile.

"We discovered we had kept the door to God closed. We saw that before we could help the world or the church, we needed help in our little world—the home. Our experience of praying together and with other couples has enriched our marriage and our family life. Our activities have taken on purpose and worth. We are happy to travel miles to share this new life and new joy."

Here is a telling letter. "It takes a little while to realize what it means to put all trust in our Lord. In church services, in Bible and devotional literature, we heard of fortunate ones who got over the hump of Christian decision and found new vistas and new beauty. We wondered, Is that for us and for our messy situation almost at the verge of divorce? We kept busy at good church works, doubting that it could be for us. Then we attended the couples meeting, and new hope arose. The people who spoke, or whose stories we heard, showed us

*is new beauty for us?*

that God has longings too, and when these longings meet at the frontier of confession and surrender in prayer, the joy is ours and must be God's also."

One more letter. "In our marriage, each of us found God, not a God who is somewhere out there, not the God of the theologians and ritual, but the God who is alive and well and dwelling in our life together. While the power of the modern world is very strong and will try to turn you into married singles, the power of God's love, working through your love for each other, can and will resist when undergirded with prayer."

*married singles?*

When we ended a recent meeting of couples discussing "marriage insurance," a prayer by Tom, who is a devoted Roman Catholic, went like this:

Lord, my policy almost lapsed last week
I read the small print, but
I haven't kept up my prayer-premiums.
Thank you for extending my period of grace.

*lapsed policies*

A policy, bought in good faith, can lapse. Separation and divorce have occurred for some couples who found new life in a prayer fellowship. When prayer ceases, the cohesive power of God's love departs.

Over the silent gulfs that appear in many marriages, the keystone of loving cooperation is put in place by the Pontifex Maximus (Supreme Bridgebuilder) of all time.

We can be grateful for the numerous studies and books that over the past fifteen years have taken the subject of human sexuality out of closets of ignorance and prudish censorship. Many, today, married—in middle-age or older —wish that they had known how to prevent or

*human sexuality*

remove psychological blocks so that sex could be fun. They have not known the "joy of sex." However, so much knowledge, openly discussed and visually portrayed, has led thousands to conclude that sex is *just* for fun—an end in itself. Norman Pittenger writes:

> Sex, like any other appetite, is a combination of purpose and pleasure. Its chief purpose is to let men and women share with God the Creator in the creative process of life. This alone keeps humanity going. As with other appetites, there goes with sex activity pleasure: intense sensual pleasure. Many do not want the responsibility that goes with the pleasure.[2]

Paul Tournier writes:

> Love has been devalued. It is but a commonplace convenience which sexes render one another, without any deep self-commitment. There is no real giving of the self.[3]

**Christian sexuality**

Does human sexuality have an advantage over Christian sexuality? Prayer power marriages that we have been considering vote no. Christian sexuality is based upon the same human need for maximum fulfillment as is essential in amoral relationships—but with several pluses.

**divine significance**

(1) Successful sex relations have divine significance, not just physical or psychological. Pittenger again writes:

> Those who are Christian believe that it is only from the Christian point of view that the fullest meaning of sexuality can be grasped—because man has a

88

certain duality: a spiritual side and a physical aspect, a temporal and an eternal aspect. He knows "eros," possessive love; he can discover "agape," self-giving love.[4]

In the atmosphere of a home grateful for God's love in Jesus Christ, the enjoyable activity of sex is another cause for gratitude (*Eucharista*). Sex is realized as a sacramental act—the outward sign of inner spiritual grace.

(2) Sex relationships in early attraction, or in climactic stages, are modes of communication. Fellowship in Christ produces the spiritual and emotional environment in which communication is open in all relationships. This includes those most delicate between husband and wife. If communication is good, sex will be better; if communication is bad, sex will not help. After a couple has had sex in different ways, they still have to get along with each other. Some of the personal attitudes that make for dysfunction in sex activity are fear of rejection, guilt, self-pity, insincerity, insensitivity, and depression.

sex is communication

Dr. Bertram Brown, psychiatrist, is assistant surgeon general of the U. S. Public Health Service. He was asked, Is there anything a depressive individual can do for himself short of seeking psychiatric help? He said, "One thing is to build into himself, before the depression begins, the idea that he is not helpless or hopeless." Help and hope, for a Christian, are more than ideas; they are motivations arising from companionship with Christ.

a good idea, but how?

"If the Son shall make you free, then are you free indeed"—for maximum sex communication.

Charlie Shedd in *Letters to Karen*, in preparation for his daughter's marriage, wrote: "In the Christian context, it is your privilege to be an angel in the home, but a devil in bed."[5]

(3) In the atmosphere of prayer together for husband and wife new lessons can be more easily learned, mistakes more easily admitted, forgiveness granted, truth frankly shared, and mutual affection deepened.

learning
continues

(4) A letter to the *New York Times* is appropriate:

> Many different influences are working to depreciate parenthood today. The women's liberation movement and the fear of a population explosion, good and necessary things, have helped make women feel a little guilty about having and raising children. Advertising and psychologizing have placed such emphasis on personal pleasure, satisfaction and "fulfillment" that it seems foolish to forego vacations, fashionable clothes and new cars for the sake of raising children.
>
> The value of parenthood, though, is inextricably tied to the value of human beings. Parenthood provides the unique opportunity to create and form a human being. The falling value given to parenthood in our society is not, I am sure, the only cause of the increase in child abuse and juvenile crime, but I can't help thinking that there is a close connection.
>
> J.C.M.
> *Hempstead, N. Y.*
> June 22, 1975

Christians take the long-range view of life and do not act in the now just for the "now." In planning for children we know the great privilege of "sharing in creation." In the wonder of conception and of birth and of caring for an amazing new life and growing personality, we are "workers together with God"—not owners but agents and trustees—with all the pain that children can bring.

> The clue to the relationship between sexual union and conception is in the word frequently used to describe it: "Procreation"—creation on behalf of another—God. Man is made for God, he is made for love.[6]

(5) Finally the word *family* has true meaning. Those in amoral arrangements may be called "couples," "partners," "experimenters," or "sposes" (do you suppose they'll ever get married?),[7] but they are not a family. Until Jesus brings us into the state-of-being-in-the-love-of-God-the-Father, we are in the state-of-being-in-the-love-of-self. Until God becomes our loving Father we have no model for other earthly relationships. We are left with only a persistent drive for personal intimacy. "Having created life, the Father, in a human family, provides fresh manifestation of himself where divine love can be at work among men."[8]

A Christian family knows its Father. He is "Our Father" because he is the "God and Father of Our Lord Jesus Christ." To know the unfathomable riches of Christ is to be prepared for the physical, emotional, and psychological responsibilities of family life—and to have a healing outreach to a broken love-of-self world.

So many couples, after discovering prayer power with honest sharing, have told me that new romance and deep sexual satisfaction had just begun—"like a honeymoon twenty years late." A divorcee said, "there is really no need for the announcement: 'those whom God has joined together, let no man put asunder!' When God continues to join, love and romance abound. I only wish I had known it earlier."

Christian marriage does not promise more than it delivers. It delivers more than we can desire or deserve.

Let us now consider the outreach of prayer power homes when joy returns to "hopeless" marriages.

the outreach

One couple found that early morning was impossible for devotions, with wife employed at the telephone company and husband, a civil engineer, off early. Late at night they were too tired. So immediately after supper they would go into their room by themselves for twenty minutes. A nine-year-old daughter and a retarded six-year-old son completed the family. After a week, the daughter asked, "What do you and mother do right after supper?"

"We pray to God out loud because we are so thankful."

"May I join you tonight?"

"gee, God, thanks a million"

Later that evening, kneeling by their side, and after their prayers, she said, "Gee, God, thanks a million."

In another home, parents had been on the verge of divorce for three years. The eight-year-old son had begun to stutter badly. Several hundred dollars had been spent on a psychologist and speech therapist. When father and mother gave themselves to Jesus Christ, they started their days with this son and two others at breakfast, reading a selected Bible passage and praying informally.

love means miracle

One morning, about six weeks later, Jack's speech cleared completely. Someone asked if I

92

did not think this a miracle. I said that I did because every time the love of God is allowed to flow in a family a miracle takes place. For three years the pollution of anger, fear, argument, or indifference had increased. Tension and insecurity had taken its toll on the family, and it had affected Jack's speech.

After a physician had given his life to God, through Christ (at three A.M.), he found that costly honesty with his wife was necessary. Asking forgiveness, he received it, and both began each day in prayer at breakfast.

His honesty at home recalled his dishonesty with some patients. "If I did not know one's ailment, I would give a prescription that would treat the symptom. This would not cure, but would keep him as my patient." *"physician, heal thyself"*

The next day, a young man came to the office. "I was surprised when God said to me, 'It's more important to cure him than to charge him.' So I suggested he go to another physician."

Later this physician phoned, "Chuck, you never sent me a patient before."

"That's right."

"Why now?"

"You see, I only became a Christian at three o'clock this morning!"

There were two other results. A new relationship developed among the four doctors in town. "With healthy relations between us now, the community is getting the best medical care."

Three months later when I saw him, I said in a light vein, "Now that you are really honest, I suppose that you have lost a lot of patients."

"On the contrary, I have more than I can handle because I now have the reputation of being a diagnostician!"

Bill, a vestryman who was the personnel director of a manufacturing concern described the change that the Holy Spirit had made in his home.

"We used to spend hours arguing, 'Who's right?' Now in prayer we ask, 'What's right?' I realized that this same Spirit was needed at the office. One morning I took with me a prayer book and put it on the desk."

"What's that for?" inquired the secretary.

"Just to make you ask that question! Betty and I have found a new start in our marriage, thanks to our newly discovered faith. I thought this whole department could stand improved relationships."

what's right?
not
who's right?

"I was wondering if you would ever wake up to see that!"

Twice a week they took part of lunch hour and each chose an appropriate prayer. One day the janitor came in to collect waste baskets and apologized for interrupting. They told him what they were doing and why. He joined.

Later a vice-president, looking for some letters, entered and found the three in prayer. He apologized. "Don't apologize. We've been praying for you." He joined.

laborers
together
with God

In a bi-monthly meeting with CIO representatives the personnel director suggested that, maybe, labor relations were like family problems—and that he had found the answer for those. Would they be willing to think about opening their meeting next time with the Lord's Prayer?

The leader said, "I'm glad you suggested that. I'm for it. I'm a preacher on Sundays. Why wait two weeks?" Thus began a new era in frankness and friendship. Disputes disappeared in the face of trust.

Several days before I left that city, Bill asked if I would like to meet some of these people. I did and count the experience among my choicest memories.

Let me tell the story of the Kemps in a different way. Ted and Marie were active church people: he was on the vestry, she was vice-president of the woman's guild.

SCENE: Rector's study, 10:00 A.M. Enter Marie.

*Marie:* Can you tell me the name of a good Christian lawyer? Ted and I want a Christian divorce.

*Rector:* I've never heard it put just that way.

*Marie:* I've decided, and Ted will not contest it. Let me tell you just what kind of a person he really is.

*Rector:* Marie, if Ted were here, he could confess his own sins. Don't you confess his. How about your own? What blocks have you put in the wall between you?

TIME LAPSE: There is the passage of about an hour during which she took a new look at her own life alongside of God's love, and of Christ's offer of forgiveness, and a new start. She came to the conclusion that her own inflexible sins of *omission* were more detrimental to their unity than his few *commissions*. The new start she wanted, and the forgiveness she needed, were hers with a full commitment to Christ and her willingness to follow the leading of the Holy

Spirit. With hope high and her imagination redirected, our conversation followed.

*Marie:* May I ask Ted to come and see you tomorrow?

*Rector:* No, and don't mention to Ted that you have been here. If he sees a difference in you he may want to know why.

*Marie:* How long do you think it might take?

*Rector:* I don't know. You said it took two years to get into this jam. Perhaps that long.

*Marie:* I can't wait that long.

*Rector:* Let me suggest something that might help. Take this pencil and pad. Relax, be quiet, and ask God to show you one thing that might surprise Ted. Write it down.

TIME LAPSE: ten minutes.

*Rector:* What came to you?

*Marie:* Two things—not just one. The first was this. "Have buckwheat cakes and sausage tomorrow for breakfast." You see, two years ago I told him I'd never serve these again—they are his favorites. Second, the Holy Spirit said, "Get a new nightgown." You see, to punish him, I have held back all sexual affection.

NEXT MORNING: 10:15 A.M. telephone rings in the rector's office.

*Ted:* Mo, this is Ted. Could I see you this afternoon?

*Rector:* Sorry, I must go out of town.

*Ted:* How about tomorrow?

*Rector:* No, some people are coming here from out of town.

*Ted:* How about Saturday?

*Rector:* Sorry I must give the whole day to sermon preparation.

*Ted:* Mo, you know you're not that busy.

*Rector:* You're right, Ted. I'm really not. Why do you want to see me?

*Ted:* You know.

*Rector:* You tell me.

*Ted:* Mo, I've got a new wife and I didn't have to go out and marry her.

Ted came that afternoon, put his past and present in God's hands and his marriage, too. Together he and Marie had paid the initial cost for a new home.

The upkeep and outreach began immediately with prayer together and a desire to share the mystery with others. (From the Greek, *mysterion* which means a "revealed secret.")

Just at that time two other couples had been contemplating divorce and had been watching what the Kemps were going to do. Their new life in Christ spread. Soon we had a team of three couples in fellowship with prayer power available to others.

On the other hand there are advocates of "divorce insurance." They note:

Current child-support awards to divorced mothers tend to be skimpy and that even so, many ex-husbands default on their obligations. "Divorce insurance" is still in the conceptual stage,

divorce
insurance

but one hypothetical formula calls for the policyholder to pay a premium of fifty dollars a year; then if the couple is divorced, support payments might amount to $100 a month for three years. The policy could cover alimony as well, in return for higher premiums. Some insurance companies have expressed tentative interest in the idea.[9]

it's a
choice

So we can take our choice: prayer power for marriage and the home, or one hundred dollars a month for three years. Insurance is essential; choose your policy.

Novels and plays are built on the eternal triangle in which husband or wife allows affection for a third person to sever their relationship. But Jesus Christ is the only third person who brings healing love with him. Here, two lovers welcome the supreme lover of all. In his eternal

life
assurance

triangle, a Christian marriage is not only insured against divorce, it is supplied with direction and resource and new romance.

We are surrounded by conflicts, pressures, and the lifestyle of cynical and nihilistic society. Death seems the only way out. But there is insurance that guarantees life—life assurance.

# prayer power for the clergy

*St. Paul to his young assistant:*
*"Beware of men in the church who preserve*
*the outward form of religion, but are standing*
*denial of its reality" (2 Tim. 3:4–5).*

IN *Fire in Coventry*, Canon Verney points out
that the commandment to "love one another" is
not new with Jesus.[1] Other religions have ex-
tolled love, but love one another "as I have
loved you" makes it new. Verney writes:

Jesus gave the Commandment just
after He had washed His friend's dirty
stinking ugly feet. You must love like
that, with a love that is humble, costly,
that comes alongside people just as
they are, that is ready to serve them.

When I was ordained I expected that
I should find myself in a new atmosphere where people loved one another. It was a shock to discover that
this was not so. Individually most
clergy are humble men who work long
hours in the service of their parishioners, but we do not, on the whole, love
one another any more than, for example, doctors or school masters. There is
the barrier of shyness and artificiality

*the*
*new*
*command-*
*ment*

that all too often we fail to break down and enter into a Christian fellowship where we accept one another as real people.

All this is terrifyingly like the world, and unlike Jesus, and is the main cause of the Church's failure to attract. For though we preach the gospel in challenging sermons, though we have deep insight into social problems and a clear grasp of the Catholic faith, though we have successful Christian Stewardship and live lives of great personal self-sacrifice, yet, if we do not love one another, all this is empty noise and worth nothing.

Shortly after a young woman was elected chairman of the church women of her diocese, she said to me in tears, "I am heart sick at the antagonisms I have found between some **clergy** priests and between priests and laymen toward **bottleneck** the bishop." Clergy, without love toward each other, are the bottleneck of the church, but clergy loving as Jesus loves, are a witness of the new life that is coming to the body of Jesus Christ.

Some time ago, five clergy were meeting, and for a change we were not having roast bishop or fried vestryman. We were asking ourselves, Why is prayer so often unreal to the professional pray-ers? Church suppers, Sunday bulletins, community service all had form and body, but not prayer. We could not blame God. All of us held specific convictions born of wrestling in prayer at seminary or at another time of decision, but these mountaintops of certainty and joy tended to be lost in the fog of "church work."

We decided to share our real feelings. We all

had great needs and shallow resources, but we looked confident enough. Materially we had sufficient, but inside somewhere we were falling apart. Barriers of churchmanship made our relationships edgy. Here and there we knew we were phony. For some, holy wedlock had become deadlock or mild neutrality. We often found our prayers orbiting around God, with no landing place. We had to admit that our petitions were unreal because in spots we were unreal. One of those spots was the temptation to be jealous. Quite often the grass on the other side of another's communion rail looks greener than mine, especially when mine is full of financial problems or personality conflicts.

*falling apart somewhere*

*jealous?*

Helen Keller wrote, "Unless we can help the world where we are, we could not help it if we were somewhere else."[2]

Besides the tendency toward jealousy, we all admitted the temptation to feel lonely. Carrying too much on our shoulders, we tried to appear confident, not in God, but in our own natural energy. We were anxious at the core. We felt distant from our wives and children and empty in relation to other clergy. Clergy need not be lonely persons; we had to admit that we let ourselves feel lonely.

*lonely?*

As one of the five said later, "When I found I could pray with my wife and other clergy, there was a new openness and warmth between us and a way out of the trap of loneliness." "Where two or three are gathered in my name, there am I in the midst of them" (Matt. 18:20).

We knew we were responsible churchmen. We found that we were not very responsive Christians. So we agreed on three things: first, that we really didn't know one another, second, that we really didn't love one another as Christ

101

loves us, and third, that we needed to pray together.

With the help of a Christian autobiography, the unknowns about each other disappeared. Religion in early childhood varied from a Jewish home, to two with tepid interest in church, to two where Jesus was friend and Lord. Confirmation at age twelve was spiritually meaningless to four. It was a real experience (as an adult) for the man of Jewish parentage.

masks off

Three out of the five had taken time out from parishes because of emotional breakdowns. We were all back now. In each case the parish had rallied around and given great spiritual and human support. Our honest answers to the question, Where do I need the grace of God now? brought us very close.

Before, I had seen each man as a professional clergyman and as a good friend. After an hour of honest sharing, for the first time we saw one another as friends of Jesus Christ. I saw a brother in need, and he saw me depending partly upon him. And whereas prayer had never happened between us, now, in prayer, there was so much to be thankful for. We could intelligently and specifically pray for the guidance of the Holy Spirit in the hurts and the joys of one another. We had reached the trust level. "Divisions that separate us are so subtle that we either do not see them or, in the light of Christ's love, find it painful to admit."[3] Yet, in that very light, and on the bridge of prayer together, we do meet.

A clergyman who found this prayer power in fellowship with other clergy said:

dishonest

> I find that one of the most difficult things is to get clergy into a fellow-

ship for informal prayer because, when clergy get together, they are a gathering of kings. Everybody has at least five old ladies who love him, no matter what he does, and they tell him so every Sunday. After a while we believe it and, when we do, then we are in trouble. When clergy meet, they are often suspicious of each other. Personal exposure threatens, but the only threat is really to our pride.

suspicious?

You know the kind of clergyman who goes around saying, "How are things going, Jack?" And he says, "Just wonderful." Inside, I feel that he is very lucky, and has a successful parish, when things are going badly for me. But when I speak to him in honesty, and get to know him, I find that things for him are not going well either.

When the fences between people are broken down and the real persons come through on a spiritual level, what I have found is that I am more united with people in failure than in success. So, when we share the things we have done wrong or when our faith and our surrender are not as they should be, there is where we become brothers in Christ.

united
in
failure

Several years ago Dr. Donald Coggan, the present archbishop of Canterbury, addressed two hundred fifty clergy in Connecticut. Speaking of the complacency of the clergy, he concluded his remarks with three pointed questions:

First, How deep is your fellowship with fellow clergy? Can you be honest, talk in depth, share your failures, your doubts, and your sins?

Second, with whom do you pray informally?

clergy
question-
naire

Many priests work well with people but do not know one another on this deeper level.

Third, do you have the same prayer fellowship with the laity where you can take criticism, or are you too proud for Christian friendship, for deep, costly, loving honesty?

In one city, and I think this may be true in general, a group of ministers had been meeting for four years every week for Holy Communion, breakfast, and a time of concern and planning for inner-city needs. Many programs had been discussed. A low-cost housing project had been originated, and some social service activities promoted. On one occasion I enjoyed their hospitality but found relationships very guarded and sometimes tense. A young assistant told me later, "If I want to speak at a meeting like that, I have to catch the eye of my pastor and get his nod." Each man had inner needs, but, hiding these, they met to get Christian activity *out into the ghetto* and *for the underprivileged.* How underprivileged can we get when Christian leaders are not able to minister to one another, be honest with one another, or pray with one another?

Many young ministers are leaving parishes after three to five years following ordination. Their families need more psychiatric care than those of older clergy. Their spiritual resources run dry very soon. One of this age said to me, "I almost left the church two years ago because I could not give to people what was expected of me as a man of God—although my diploma said I was equipped to do it. I could and did give other things. I was a youth organizer. I made hospital calls. I knew the Bible and preached it. I marched for righteous causes. But

*(margin note)* under-
privileged

I could not give or share what I had not yet fed upon. The whole world of prayer was an unknown tongue to me.

"What a shell I have been building around myself. But now, with the grace of Our Lord, and in his company, with openness at home and with a growing number of clergy, I am off on 'project unlimited.'"

In one city seven clergy in downtown churches met twice a month for lunch and general discussion about parish and area needs. When honest one day, they admitted that they were really sparring with each other because they did not know the others' real hurts, hungers, and hang-ups.

The agenda for the next meeting was scrapped. Christian autobiographies emerged, and prayer together began.

One of the seven said, "After five years in the ministry, I was a clergy dropout. I left to work with a large electronics company. They gave me the eight-month course to get acquainted with all parts of the industry. I was a junior executive. With that idea and with sufficient salary, I bought a Mercedes Benz. It looked as if we had it made.

clergy
dropout

"However, I did have to think. I realized that I was in something that was not big enough to believe in, to invest all the rest of my life and energy. When I left the ministry, I blamed the church, but I came to admit that I was 90 percent of the trouble.

"I came to realize that I had gone to the seminary unconverted, had been ordained unconverted, and had been trying to make a Christian parish 'go' with an unconverted leader. In business now my hunger for Jesus Christ was 'for real.' A great loneliness was mine because I had not yet committed my life to him. I was so miserable that when I shaved I would make faces at myself in the mirror. It was so empty to be in something I didn't believe in.

"I longed to be back. I said, 'Lord, I know now you've got me. What shall I do about it?'

back with joy

"I resigned without talking to anyone but Betty. There was no church eager to take me on. The Mercedes went first, and with it, happily, the weight of what had been a status symbol of success. In the course of three months, 'God for real' revealed himself. It happened in a small mission parish, poor in looks and poor in people, with the minister's house unattractive at all times and draughty in winter. But Betty and I were, for the first time, free, at peace, and happy."

Father Neil Hurley, a Jesuit, speaking of the way to Christian reunion has said:

where to begin

All of us must cease picking at the church's sore spots and allow a healing process to begin. There are problems: tradition, authority, and narrowness, but if we temporarily put them on the shelf, or leave them to others, *and begin with our unhealed selves and relationships,* we may create the atmosphere in which right change and reformation of structure will bear the most fruit.

love as I have loved you

There is a legend that during a clergy meeting Jesus entered the room and said, "A new commandment I give to you."

The Methodist said, "Is it moral?"

The Lutheran said, "Is it reformed?"

The Presbyterian said, "Is it intellectual?"

The Pentecostal said, "Is it ecstatic?"
The Episcopalian said, "Is it traditional?"
The Roman Catholic said, "Is it ecumenical?"
And, as he left the room, someone heard him say, "Forget it, boys!"

# 10

# prayer power for the church

*The church seems to have taught people
how to be good humanitarians.
Perhaps, if it tried hard,
it could make them good Christians.*

IS THE RESTRUCTURING of much in the church going to do away with the parish and the congregation? Are we so top-heavy or brittle that we must start all over again with the "simple gospel"?

Loren Mead in his *New Hope for Congregations* doesn't think so. "The parish is here to stay. Congregations survive catastrophes. They bob to the surface after revolutions, plagues, and counterrevolutions. They live under persecutions and they live on when pampered or protected."

the parish
is here
to stay

He does have some concerns. "I do not worry about the survival of local congregations. I do worry about the quality of the parish that survives, and what we can do about it. Today I see Christians living in a kind of bondage in their parishes, estranged from what they want to be, from each other, and from the world."[1]

This is our concern too. It is a joy to know that a release from bondage is offered, not primarily in the realm of changing parish structures, but in the changing lives of parishioners.

The power of God and the Holy Spirit is binding Christians in honesty, mutual prayer, and love. Familiar church work, formalities, false faces, spiritual unreality, and lifeless service need no longer be the parish image. Rather, "Men will know you are my disciples if you love one another as I have loved you."

We believe that those who have stopped worshiping with the church would secretly like to be convinced that what we say with our lips, we believe in our hearts and show forth in our lives.

In West Virginia, a census taker was wondering how to reach a cabin high on a mountain. He met a youngster and asked, "Do you live around here?"

"Yep, up in that cabin."

"Good, is your daddy home?"

"He's in the pen."

"Is your mother home?"

"Nope, she's in the house of correction."

"Do you have a brother?"

"Yep."

"Where is he?"

"He's at Harvard."

"Harvard! What's he studying?"

"He ain't studying nothing, mister. They're studying him."

people study us

In a very real sense those of us who go to church, support the church, or say our prayers are being studied. What real difference does our faith make? Many parishes have been asking that question. Several years ago representatives of the Anglican communion launched "Mutual Responsibility and Interdependence Is the Body of Christ," hoping to show the difference it does make. In the first chapter of the study manual was the question, Is what we are now doing, advancing the cause of the church of Jesus Christ? That is, what should we be doing to have men know the risen Lord?

In one parish we wrestled with the question and agreed that we should be doing more: modernize the liturgy, investigate inner-city problems, increase missionary giving, and do more for the poor. And then someone suggested dropping out the word *doing* and phrasing the question this way: Is what we are now, advancing the cause of the church of Jesus Christ? *"Is what we are, now?"* What of our corporate spirit, not our activity? What of our relationships within the parish family? What of our Christian community? Are we a corporate witness of what happens when Christ is real, when love is real, and when God the Holy Spirit guides in prayer? Could it be that in doing things that matter greatly we have been neglecting the one thing that matters most? Isn't it easier to do something *for* God, than to do something *with* him?

**what are we now?**

God calls us first to be, then to behave according to who we are.

John Higgins, while bishop of Rhode Island, said:

> The evangelical finds no evidence in Scripture that man can be transformed by altering his environment. Christians from a liberal background need to ponder this seriously lest they fall down and worship the god of environment which is a major fallacy of Marxism and some others. Let us not be so articulate on the active edge that we are silent at the vitalizing center in the human soul where commitment to Jesus Christ begins.

110

Activists can change a system, but they tend to leave self-centered man unchanged. In the same manner, higher educators regard men, not as sinners needing rebirth, but as basically nice people who only need encouragement, self-confidence, information, and culture.

Prayer is not inactivity; prayer is to be where the action is, that is, where *God's action* is.[2] His action is to supply compassion, love, direction, and communication. How many there must be who are giving the cup of cold water without knowing the refreshment of living water in prayer. And how many there must be who are giving the loaf of bread without feeding on the bread of life. If there is nutritional poverty in our country and starvation in the world, there is a greater poverty of faith among the well-fed, and they seem ignorant of their malnutrition. If there is pollution of rivers, there is the greater pollution of aimlessness, boredom, nihilism, and fear. And if there is a shortage of nature's power, there is a greater shortage of prayer power. "Christian activity is not a goal, it is a consequence."[3] Christians go with joy to the place of prayer, but Henri le Seux says that they go away from it with the same joy "for we do not leave God's Presence when we plunge into the duties of the day."[4]

On the night before an all-day workshop in a large city parish, I met with eight women who had been on the committee for a year's self-study of that parish. They had spent time at parish life conferences and training sessions. They had read volumes about the church and the inner city. They had listened to experts on the urban church.

I asked about the results of their self-study. They said that their problems could be summed

*prayer is action*

where does
a church
begin
self-study?
up in one word, *communication*—communication between bishop and diocesan commissions, between the bishop and clergy, between clergy and between the clergy and laity, and between laity and laity in the congregation. I asked what they recommended as a result of all this time and energy.

They listed certain structural simplifications, changes in the education curriculum, more efficient methods of parish financing, and the like. Then I asked, "How far in your *self-study* did you go to evaluate your relationships with each other as Christians at the various conferences? Did you take each other for granted and begin with the problems of the inner-city church?" I pointed out that not one of their structural changes had to do with communication between the church's leaders and added, "Here among you eight, do you know each other on the Christian level of praying informally with one another? Do you love each other that much?" This

where
"church
work"
begins
was an entirely new thought to these active, sincere church leaders, namely, that "church work" really begins with caring enough about each other to assist one another in the spiritual life of prayer.

In studying their situation, they had stressed dialogue, and dialogue is good up to a point. In dialogue, we can keep our real selves, our needs, our hopes, our weaknesses to ourselves. We can safely keep on the level of ideas and hide from each other. In dialogue, there is just my side and your side. Dialogue may well result in

from
dialogue
to
trialogue
change for better structures, but prayer power raises us from dialogue to *trialogue*. In trialogue there is still my side and your side, but there is the side of the Holy Spirit who, as we listen in prayer, first shows us blocks in ourselves that

make love of no effect. In trialogue, we find the essential change needed is not in outer structures so much as in the inner strictures of our souls—dishonesties, dislikes, discouragements, insincerities, and respectable lusts. Situations will change as people are changed, as men, women, and youth come into a liberating relationship with Jesus Christ and with each other. It is not so much that prayer changes things, as that prayer changes people, and people change things.

structures
or
strictures

There must be structures and there must be systems; there is no case for anarchy. But every structure carries in it the seeds of its own destruction, whether a state, a church, or a social program—none of which can love or be loved. One's allegiance to any system must be considered in light of the greater need of one's neighbor. Let us not dismiss the need of changes in our distorted structures so that justice and economic opportunity and fairness to all will be achieved. Man is greater than any social unit of which he is a component part. Therefore, his need for personal meaning is essential if the social units are to have social meaning.

So, the eight VIP's took time for quiet. They sought God's guidance to remove any blocks between them. When we prayed in a circle a little later, there were eight prayers offered out loud. The committee members discovered a joyful bond had been forged among them by God's spirit on a level that was miles above that of good friendship or of activity with church people. Later one of them said of the others, "Before, I thought I knew the group—we had worked together in the church for years. Now it is clear that we had really been strangers."

no
longer
strangers

The objective is not only, and not primarily, to bring into being groups for Bible study, for healing, and for prayer fellowship. These can become "Holy Huddles." But the purpose is to see the love that results in existing church organizations when these activities are peopled (and the community served) by an increasing number of persons in a prayer relation with God and each other.

A new rector came to a small congregation that had no choir. Two parishioners, within a few days of each other, volunteered to help start a choir. To each, he said, "Yes, we should have one, but we want a choir with singers who know the Lord and who can pray together as well as practice and sing together." The first volunteer claimed that this was not the way to get the best singers. The second parishioner accepted the minister's challenge and discovered a rich faith in Christ. An excellent volunteer choir resulted that not only produced musical harmony but set a spiritual harmony that influenced the parish as a whole.

choir

Sunday school teachers and pupils who spend time in quiet and prayer together before dismissal remember each other during the week. They begin each day in prayer for one another.

Sunday school

The purpose of a weekly church staff meeting should be more than oiling the organizational wheels. Clergy, organist, secretary, and sexton can "bear one another's burdens."

staff

> A small group has more to do with relationships than with structure. Any group situation can be the setting in which persons are supported, set free, and equipped for effective living. Yours may be a committee with an agenda, a mission group with a job, or a fellow-

ship group primarily concerned about its own members. *Whatever the form, whatever happens to the people involved is more important than group structures or work accomplished.*[5]

A rector said to his vestry, "Instead of my opening with a prayer, I suggest that we begin with a time of quiet after which each one may express his own concerns to God." He told me, "I knew one man could and would participate in this informal prayer. I was surprised when three others thanked God for something, or prayed for the sick, or for me."

After several months, all were being bound together in prayer that expressed their deep problems or joys. Their wives said, "We are delighted because vestry meetings now are at least thirty minutes shorter." The reason was that time was not wasted with minor items. The quiet at the opening removed all negative attitudes, one for another in the vestry.

In another parish where informal prayer is part of the vestry agenda for the opening and closing of a meeting, the meeting may be interrupted by prayer! The rector explained, "If a sticky problem arises, we pray about it. Unless the vote is unanimous, we pray about it, and then see where we are. If there isn't a consensus, we table it until there is. It is still God's church. He will handle it."

An adult confirmation class included prayer, not only as a study, but with extemporaneous prayer around. The rector said that there were numerous Protestant church persons in this class, and they were delighted that they would not have to drop their informal praying which they had known in other communions simply because they were coming into a church that

*[margin notes: vestry meetings; prayer power in parishes; adult classes]*

used a prayer book. One woman about thirty-one asked, "May I sing my prayer?" At the next meeting she brought her guitar, and for the duration of the course, she sang, and all learned a new song each week. The rector said, "You know, I believe I must have the swingingest confirmation class in the diocese."

After an all-day workshop for clergy and laity, nine clergy decided to meet regularly on Fridays for a closer sense of Christian fellowship. After five weeks when the attendance reached twenty, the dean wrote about three developments.

clergy
from
9 to 20

> The atmosphere is beginning to clear. We are amazed at the dispelling of prejudging, jealousy, and sensitiveness. We feel so close to Christ. Hostility is beginning to melt though it hasn't gone completely. In the second place, our outlook on the diocese is clearing. We are beginning in this area to work as a team. And in the third place, we feel closer to the bishop because we are praying for him daily, as well as for each other. Some of our number didn't know him too well. Some had erroneous ideas about him, and we were able to dispel these. Last week when he visited the parish, he commented on the warmth among clergy and laymen.

We must not leave out prayer power in the rectory. Most clergy and their wives do not pray together very easily. But if depth of honesty and forgiving love and mutual prayer is important in any Christian home, is it not imperative in a rectory where the occupational hazards include sensitiveness, professionalism, resentment, and loneliness? The personal and

in the
rectory

parental relationships there give hope or distress to families within the parish.

The wife of a clergyman wrote that she and her husband could see no way out of their misery except divorce. "I came to the point where I had to say, 'I've had it!'" Then she met a woman who said that once she had felt the same way but had discovered that the loving Jesus Christ stands at every wit's end. In letting her own hurt feelings, rebellion, and despair be absorbed by God's love, she wrote, "I can now, with victory, write 'I've had it'—I've had his new start in my own soul and, with Jack, great joy in prayer together which spiritually lubricates the home."

"I've had it"

A clergyman told this story. "When we were married, my wife gave me a prayer desk. It was big enough for two. For fifteen years it has been with us in two parishes. It was carefully moved to new rectories. It has been regularly polished, but not until Friday have we used the prayer desk together, kneeling and honestly sharing with each other our hidden needs, our real hurts and feelings. How close Christ's arms have been felt! How different the rectory looked the next morning. And instead of a sermon on Sunday, I shared the new hope I have for our family and for all the families in the parish."

the prayer desk

The district, the presbytery, or the diocese—the larger ecclesiastical units—have also found renewed spiritual energy through prayer power.

I asked an American bishop, "Whom do you feel free to call upon and to pray with within your diocesan house?"

He said, "With no one. We do have noonday prayers in the chapel, led by one of the staff, but that's not what you are talking about, is it?"

In another diocese there were three parishes

in close proximity with very alive prayer groups. At a joint meeting it was suggested they ask the bishop to meet with them. He was phoned and asked if he was free to see representatives of three parishes. There was a pause.

"What's wrong?" he asked.

are you there, bishop?

"Nothing at all, bishop, we just want to see you and to pray with you and to pray for the diocese."

Again silence. "Are you there, bishop?"

"Oh, yes," he said, "but I must tell you that though I have been asked to see parishioners for problems with their clergy or problems of finance, this is the first time in twelve years as a bishop I have been asked to meet a group for prayer."

Several days later ten persons spent an hour with him, each sharing what their new prayer life meant personally and together. He shared times of real need and the support of God in prayer. As they left, he remarked, "If this could happen in every parish in my diocese, my work would have so much more joy."

God breaking through, through prayer

Bishop Bardsley of Coventry said, "I see this great weapon of prayer affecting a whole diocese," and it eventually did. But it began with a small prayer group, just two, the bishop and Canon Verney. As it spread among the clergy with honest sharing, informal praying, and a new joy, he said, "What a relief to see, Anglo-Catholics, Evangelicals, and Modernists becoming friends." And he concluded, "Prayer! God breaking through, through prayer!"

# 11

# Spirit, Son, and Father

*They will know we are Christians*
*by our love.*

WILLIAM TEMPLE said that Christianity is "the most materialistic of all the great religious faiths."[1] This is not to imply that Christianity develops *materialists*. Rather, the statement refers to the fact that, in Jesus, God became man, of the material of flesh and blood. As other creatures, he had to depend upon the earth and sun for food and breath, and ultimately he knew pain and death. He took water as initiation in baptism. He took bread and wine in thanksgiving and made these basic materials vehicles for continuous thanksgiving (Eucharist) in remembering him (recalling, calling him back).

Christian
materialism

We are familiar with *incarnation* as applied to the body of the Son of God and its nine months' preparation. What we forget is that God the Father is incarnate, that is, revealed in another body—his whole creation.*

God's
three
bodies

At Pentecost there is a third incarnation, new

* Romans 1:20.

119

life in a body of believers. Over a two- to three-year period Jesus prepared a small group to be the Holy Ghost's vehicle in which to "live and move and have his being" out in the world. The Holy Spirit has continually revealed the love of Creator and Redeemer in the uniting of his disciples in the fellowship—the *koinonia*, the church. Bishop Temple wrote, "Christ wrote no book. He left in the world a body of men on whom the Spirit came. There was nothing stereotyped. The Living Society—the Church, was to be the primary witness."[2]

In theology, we seek reasoned orderliness. We put God the Father first because he started everything. We put God as incarnate in Jesus second because he came later "in the fullness of time" (just the right time). We put God the Holy Spirit last because Pentecost followed the nativity by about thirty years.

God: "three-personal"

The order in which we express our Christian belief in God—"our three-personal" God (which expression C. S. Lewis prefers to the *Trinity*[3]) —is from Matthew's account of Jesus' command to his disciples. He commissioned them to go into the whole world to teach all nations and to baptize men into the Good News community, his continuing Body, "in the name of Father, Son, and Holy Spirit."

A good many people nowadays say, "I believe in God, but not in a personal God." They feel that the mysterious something which is behind all other things must be more than a person. Now the Christians quite agree, but they are the only people who offer any idea of what a being that is beyond personality could be like. Others, though they say that God is *beyond* personality, really think of him as something impersonal, that is, as something *less* than personal. "If you are looking for something super-personal, something *more* than a person, then it isn't a question of choosing between the Christian idea and the other ideas. The Christian idea is the only one on the market."[4]

Someone criticized the creeds for only making mention of the Holy Spirit. He said, "God is described as Almighty Father and Creator of all that is visible and invisible. The Son's biography is outlined from his conception, and before, to Calvary and beyond, to the place of Glory, but the Spirit is just mentioned in passing."

the
Holy Spirit
in
the creeds

I said, look again. The Holy Spirit comes from the Father. He is Lord and continuing life-giver. Furthermore, he is personally concerned about us. In fact, in the third paragraph of the creed we find ourselves. Through the Spirit, we are built into the body of Christ (One, Holy, Catholic, and Apostolic) on earth,[5] then beyond, in the communion of the saints. So true and joyous is this fellowship of the Holy Spirit that we keenly "look for" the life of the world to come.

Dr. Pitney Van Dusen, in his rich study of the Holy Spirit, titled *The Spirit, the Son, and the Father*,[6] inverts the familiar order for a very convincing reason. If we, as pagans, had lived in the first hundred or two hundred years of the Christian excitement, we would have been drawn to it (or repelled) because of the joyful spirit, warm affection, and fearless courage of believers whom we might have found in small groups throughout the Roman world. It was so obvious that they loved each other, and they reached out to all others. Even if reviled, they did not hate in return. Our curiosity would have been high; we would have been surprised that these Christians had a new spirit we could not explain. They knew a sustaining power, a joy, a wholeness, and a peace within. They had found the courage to face life with certainty and delight which the world just could not take away.

**the joyless pagan world**

William Barclay, in *The Promise of the Spirit*, writes:

> There was no joy in the pagan world apart from the growing Christian fellowship. The pagan world was desperately aware of sin, and at the same time, it was desparingly aware that there was no possible way from sin to goodness. It was conscious of a disease for which there was no possible cure. There was no one and nothing to whom it could turn for renewal. Seneca wrote, "We have all sinned, some less, some more. We have not stood bravely enough by our good resolutions. It is not only that we have done wrong, we shall do so to the end."
>
> Here is what the Holy Spirit offered to a world where the foundations were shaking, because the Holy Spirit is He who enables us to identify ourselves with God, through Jesus Christ.[7]

This joy and confidence surprised the pagan world.

The jailer at Philippi must have been typical of those surprised. Paul and Silas, beaten with whips, sat in their cell and sang most of the night. They knew prayer power together and thanked God for the privilege of being his chosen servants. Continuous praise must have bothered the tough jailer, but the Spirit behind it finally "got" him. He didn't know the reason.

When he could "take it" no longer, he came and pleaded, "Men, how do you get this way?" or as Luke puts it, "What must I do to be saved?" His question was like Dante's demand to Virgil in *The Inferno*, "Give me the food for which you have already given me the appetite."[8]

Their faith was certain. They gave a direct reply, "Believe on the Lord Jesus Christ."

They were not like the seminary professor, an expert on discussion groups, who was asked the same question and replied, "Now that is an interesting question. What would you say? Perhaps we can get a resource person."

Dr. Van Dusen points out that the Holy Trinity was not taught theologically but discovered personally. *By viewing the life and fellowship of the Holy Spirit in the church, pagans were led to discover the grace of our Lord Jesus Christ and, through him, to know the love of the Father.*

It has been true, through the ages, that the surprise of Christian love and joy, shown especially through hardships, created in pagans a hunger which was only satisfied in fellowship with our triune God: Spirit, Son, and Father. This new life in the Body is being spread the same way.

Looking at the men and women, the young people in school and college whose experiences we have recounted, we can see that, over and over, "surprise" has been the vehicle of the Holy Spirit. There was the surprise of "church work" beginning with a praying relationship, of the atomic scientist effecting relationships in a university lab. And there was the surprise of a college professor declining a more lucrative

*(margin notes)* surprised by joy

*(margin notes)* surprised today

appointment—a personnel director suggesting
prayer as the secret weapon for cooperation in
labor-management relations—one physician surprising another by being honest and the medical quality of a community being raised. Young
people in prayer fellowship surprising parents,
and vice versa. As true a surprise today as in
the first century: "See how these Christians love
one another!"

Dr. Van Dusen shows that by the fourth century the niceties of dogmatic theology had almost squeezed the life out of the Christian
gospel. Over the centuries, other influences have
neutralized the spiritual experience: ritualism,
political power, wealth, and greed. Even sub-
stitution of good works has thwarted the life of
the Spirit, but, like a river that will not be held
back forever behind a dam, God's Spirit has,
through the ages, broken through human barriers or circumvented them.

Are we not in such a time in history? I be-
**surprised**  lieve that in the very midst of the bankruptcy
**tomorrow**  of materialism and humanism, of the murky
gloom of atheism, of widespread use of escape
drugs, of broken homes without religion, of
political amorality and of violence, discord, and
confusion of human bondage, we can thank
God we are privileged to live.[9]

I know it is true in the growth of small cells
of prayer with relationships changed by Jesus
Christ. I have seen it in the renewed awaken-
ing to spiritual healing and, cutting across all
communions, in charismatic joy.

We detect an air of surprise growing across
the land and around the world. God, through
his Spirit, is changing lives. The question is
again being asked, How do you get that way?

## Surprise

Our God might have kept his love to himself,
His caring he might have hid;
But he couldn't, you see, because, in truth,
He wouldn't be love if he did.

How great a surprise to a suffering thief
When a remembrance would suffice:
A promise came from the central cross
The gift of paradise!

Pilate and Herod to bed that night,
Certain of victory won.
What a surprise on Pentecost
Their troubles, just begun.

The jailor of Paul at Philippi
Heard him joyfully sing and pray
That "bugged" him—in surprise he asked,
"How do you get that way?"

God's children, who do not see him for real,
Will only open their eyes
When they, too, question why? and how?
Our lives are such a surprise!

# postscript

Unfortunately, many important aspects of prayer have had to be left out. Private prayer and corporate prayer are included; but the missing link between them, the vital link between Christians—a small fellowship in prayer—has been our focus because it is missing in most of our churches.

Those deeply concerned with bodily healing may be disappointed, but you will find a vast amount of reading material on this topic. Actually everything we have written has been about healing: bringing health and new cells of health to the sickest body in the world—the body of Christ, his church.

Pentecostals will miss terms like *baptism in the Spirit* or *speaking in tongues.* There are an increasing number of available publications devoted to this form of prayer. Our purpose has been to try to praise the Lord in one tongue and to give evidence of the new life of the Holy Spirit in small reconciling groups whose witness for Jesus Christ to the world is in loving one another.

# suggestions for small groups

The following ideas and procedures have been found helpful in starting or enriching small groups. Here is a sample format for a Koinonia (fellowship) Group. It combines study, sharing, and prayer.

## STRUCTURE

### Number of Persons
Twelve people is an ideal small-group size. Meetings are held in homes, and each is led by a different member.

### Purpose
To deepen one's experience with Jesus Christ and to know his life in community.

### Number of Sessions
As many as there are chapters in the book chosen for study.

## PROGRAM

### Study
Choose a book. Each member should read through the entire book; then the group can concentrate on one chapter a week. *Prayer Power* can be used in this manner over a ten-week period.

### Sharing One's Discoveries
The leader opens with a prayer and reports what the chapter said to him, perhaps reading aloud some paragraphs. In turn, each member of the group shares his

or her discoveries (5 minutes each). *One is not interrupted; there is no discussion.* Admittedly, this approach is contrary to the emphasis on dialogue, but an amazing thing happens—*each member learns to listen.*

### Quiet and Prayer

When all have pooled their insights and observations, take time for quiet, reflection, and meditation. End with vocal or silent prayer. If one prays silently, let him say "amen" when finished, so the next member may know when to start. It will not be long before all will be praying out loud.

### Final Meeting

This can be a special occasion marked by a home communion service and each group member's rededication to Christ.

### For Growth and Fellowship

If keen interest and fellowship continue, divide the group. Each six get another six, and begin again.

(For further information on Koinonia Groups, see Robert Raines, *New Life in the Church* [New York: Harper & Row, 1961]).

*Prayer Power* may also be used for study classes or special meetings.

The Centrality of Jesus Christ—Chapter 2
The Lord's Prayer—Chapter 3
Sin, Forgiveness, and Freedom—Chapters 4 and 5
For Marriage Counseling—Chapters 6 and 7
For Clergy Convocations—Chapters 8 and 9
For Evangelism—Chapter 10

The following suggestions and questions will help give structure to the meeting and prepare one before coming to a meeting.

## Suggestions for Small Groups

CHAPTER 1
1. From whom do I hide? Why?
2. Do we know each other *as Christians?*
3. Will we begin with a Christian autobiography?
4. After a time of quiet, pray aloud for the person on your right.

CHAPTER 2
1. Bishop Hines defines the gospel as "what has happened in me." What is *my* gospel?
2. Dr. E. Stanley Jones lists loneliness, laziness, lust, and lack of purpose as campus problems. Are any of these mine?
3. What is the difference between believing *that* and believing *in?*
4. What did Bishop Powell say was God's problem? Where am I tempted to resist his love?

CHAPTER 3
1. Why are we immature if we do not pray?
2. Which part of the Lord's Prayer applies to a present need of mine?
3. How have I been satisfying my six basic needs?
4. Have I thought God's will unfair? Am I prone to self-pity?
5. Think of one area in which we have been praying for God's help. Will we say, "Lord, I'll help you here"?

CHAPTER 5
1. Does the Bible have a place in my day? Do I relax and listen?
2. What idols eclipse the Son of God?
3. Am I acting like a sub-Christian martyr?
4. In what areas am I praying too hard?

CHAPTER 6
1. Do I forgive? Have I forgotten?
2. When guilty, what do I do? Evade, try to forget, cover-up, condemn myself?

3. Why would a garbage can be appropriate in the sanctuary?
4. Take time for quiet. Pray around, then pass the peace.

CHAPTER 7

1. Is my blueprint for personal relationships that of Jesus on Calvary—his eternal triangle?
2. Do my relationships end at death?
3. In my family is there a generation gap or regeneration victory?
4. What difference would prayer make for an engaged couple?

Friendship grows from interest in a common object.

It's possible to reach a human objective, go beyond it, and drift apart.

It's possible to grow toward a common objective, then move into a parallel and tepid existence.

In Christian marriage any Mary and John, committed to Jesus Christ, move nearer and become dearer to each other. But we find him always moving toward us. So we love because he loves us.

In the church, his body, the personal triangle becomes the wheel of the larger family.

There is continuation of prayer relationship when some leave the church on earth for the church in paradise—the communion of saints.

CHAPTER 8

1. In our life assurance policy, how do we read the small print? What are the continuing premiums?
2. With which home situation do I identify?
3. If you would add informal prayer at home to your private and corporate worship, try this:

On the front of a sheet of paper list 1, 2, and 3 vertically, leaving about 2 inches between numerals. Do the same on the back of the page.

Alongside the numerals on the front, write a trait or attitude in which you know you fail and which if changed would be a pleasant surprise to your mate.

Now, turn the sheet over and trade it for your spouse's paper. Without reading the other's list, write alongside 1, 2, and 3 the traits or attitudes of your spouse which if changed would greatly delight you. Fold the papers and keep them until you are ready to retire in the evening.

Kneeling together before the Lord, use this honest account as a prayer guide, seeking forgiveness or courage or new love. Someone has said, "When you look at that paper, you had *better* pray."

A couple, using this simple formula, discovered a new way to live each day. She said, "I can't tell you how our praying together has affected Fred's life and mine—all the way through to sex. The past three months had been a nightmare with self-pity and bitterness mounting. Though we were regular at worship and busy in parish activities, there was coldness and irritation and loneliness in our home. We could see no way out, but now we know why Jesus is the way, why his way reveals the truth; and we know he supplies life."

131

Fred said, "Now that things are all right in our marriage, they go all right all day in business and with friends."

Couples, try the suggestions above.

Singles, what change in me would surprise and delight members of my family?

Take time for quiet and for prayer. Make intercessions for newly married and for homes threatened with separation or divorce.

CHAPTER 9

1. For Clergy: What spoke to me in this section? Use Archbishop Coggan's questions.
2. For Laity: Do I pray daily for my minister? Does he know it? Have I asked him to pray with me?

CHAPTER 10

1. Is what we are (doing) advancing the cause of the church of Jesus Christ?
2. Where does our "church work" begin?
3. Do we dialogue or trialogue? Are we beginning with structures or strictures?
4. Are clergy wives left out of prayer power?
5. Where is "this great weapon of prayer" forged?

CHAPTER 11

1. What surprised pagans in apostolic days?
2. Might the Holy Spirit use me to surprise another? My minister (if I am a layman)? My congregation (if I am ordained)?
3. Looking back, thank God for a richer understanding of him and of one another.
4. Looking ahead, consider a home Holy Communion next week. Shall we continue with another six- to eight-week study and fellowship? Is it time to divide and extend the original group?

# notes

*Chapter 2*

1. William Barclay, *The Promise of the Spirit* (London: Wyvern Books, 1964), p. 113.

2. J. B. Phillips, *Making Men Whole* (New York: Macmillan, 1953), p. 25.

3. In a letter from Ernest Gordon.

4. G. H. A. Studdert-Kennedy, *The Sorrows of God* (New York: Doran, 1924), p. 17.

5. John A. T. Robinson, *Honest to God* (Philadelphia: Westminster, 1963).

6. William Morris, *The American Heritage Dictionary of the English Language* (New York: McGraw, 1969), p. 1529. With appreciation to Prof. Bard McNulty of Trinity College, Hartford, Conn.


*Chapter 3*

1. Paul Tournier, *The Meaning of Gifts* (Richmond, Va.: John Knox Press, 1970), p. 31.

2. *U. S. News and World Report*, Sept. 29, 1975.

3. Alex Carrel, "Prayer Is Power," *Foreword*, p. 3.

4. Although I believe this to be so, we cannot omit holiness, for there is too much in the Old Testament and in the New Testament about God's holiness and man's fulfillment.

Mother Teresa, caring for the destitute in Calcutta, speaks of holiness: "Our progress towards holiness depends upon God's grace and our will to be holy, by accepting whatever he gives us, and giving whatever he takes from us. True holiness consists in doing God's will with a smile" (Malcolm Muggeridge, *Something Beautiful for God;* Fortune Books, 1972, p. 60).

In *A Diary of Private Prayer,* John Baillie writes:
"Teach me, O God, to use all the circumstances of my
life today, that they may bring forth in me the fruits of
holiness, rather than the fruits of sin:

Let me use disappointment as material for patience
Let me use success as material for thankfulness
Let me use suspense as material for perseverance
Let me use danger as material for courage
Let me use reproach as material for long-suffering
Let me use praise as material for humility
Let me use pleasures as material for temperance, and
Let me use pain as material for endurance." (New
York: Scribner's, 1949), p. 101.

5. Carrel, "Prayer Is Power," *Foreword,* p. 3.

6. St. Theresa of Avila.

*Chapter 5*

1. Dag Hammarskjøld, *Markings* (New York: Knopf,
1964), p. 56.

2. William Barclay, *The Promise of the Spirit* (London: Wyvern Books, 1964), p. 125.

3. Mother Teresa of Calcutta.

4. *The Living Church,* 13 April 1975, p. 12.

5. Studdert-Kennedy, *The Sorrows of God,* p. 27.

*Chapter 6*

1. See Karl Menninger, *Whatever Happened to Sin?*
(New York: Hawthorn, 1973).

2. Ann Landers, *Hartford Courant,* 14 November 1974.

3. A line from Edwards and Stone's musical *1776.*

4. Robert Collins, *Journal of the American Medical Association,* April 26, 1975.

5. Michel Quoist, *I've Met Jesus Christ* (New York:
Doubleday, 1973), p. 11.

6. Benjamin Spock, *Raising Children in a Difficult
Time* (New York: Norton, 1974).

7. Richard Robertiello, *Newsweek,* 21 October 1974.

8. Compare this with Luke 18:1, "Men ought always
to pray."

9. *The Living Church*, 20 January 1974.

10. W. Irving Harris, Princeton, N. J.

11. *The Living Church*, 23 January 1973.

12. Homer *Iliad* 1.37–41. Appreciation to Professor John Williams, Trinity College, Hartford, Conn.

13. Over a six-year span we had prayer power workshops in ten states. After presenting the subject, "Obstacles to Prayer," we would divide into small groups to see if we identified with the obstacles listed and to list others that might be particularly personal. Believe it or not, seventy-two were added! Here are a few: pride, fear, worry, the hold of possessions, half-forgiving, half-confessed sin, fear of criticism, grief, impatience, unwillingness to listen to prayer (God might tell me something I don't want to hear), and despair. These are all quite respectable sins.

### Chapter 7

1. Paul Tournier, *The Meaning of Gifts* (Richmond, Va.: John Knox Press, 1963). See also these books by Dr. Tournier: *The Whole Person in a Broken World* (New York: Harper & Row, 1964), *Escape From Loneliness* (Philadelphia: Westminster, 1962), *The Meaning of Persons* (New York: Harper & Row, 1957).

### Chapter 8

1. Services For Trial Use, Episcopal Church.

2. Norman Pittenger, *A Christian View of Human Sexuality* (New York: Seabury Press, 1954), pp. 20–21.

3. Tournier, *The Meaning of Gifts* (Richmond, Va.: John Knox Press, 1963), pp. 32 and 35.

4. Pittenger, *A Christian View of Human Sexuality*, p. 34.

5. Charlie Shedd, *Letters to Karen* (Nashville: Abingdon, 1965).

6. Pittenger, *A Christian View of Human Sexuality*, p. 25.

7. Jane Otten, "Living in Syntax," *Newsweek*, 30 December 1974, p. 9.

8. Pittenger, *A Christian View of Human Sexuality*, p. 29.

9. *Newsweek*, 29 January 1972.

*Chapter 9*

1. Stephen Verney, *Fire in Coventry* (Old Tappan, N. J.: Fleming H. Revell, 1964), p. 55.

2. Helen Keller, *My Religion* (New York: Pyramid Publication, 1974), p. 101.

3. *A Common Discipline* (Coventry Cathedral).

*Chapter 10*

1. Loren Mead, *New Hope for Congregations* (New York: Seabury Press, 1973), p. 125.

2. Helen Shoemaker, *Prayer Is Action* (New York: Morehouse-Barlow, 1969).

3. Allen W. Brown, Bishop of Albany, retired.

4. The Forward Movement, July 9, 1975.

5. *Guidelines for Groups* (Columbia, Md.: Faith At Work).

*Chapter 11*

1. William Temple, *Readings in Saint John's Gospel* (New York: Macmillan, 1940), p. xx.

2. Ibid., p. xxi.

3. C. S. Lewis, *Beyond Personality* (London: Geoffrey Blas, 1944), pp. 13–17.

4. Ibid.

5. "One; because it is one Body under one Head;
   Holy; because the Holy Spirit dwells in it, and sanctifies its members;
   Catholic; because it is universal, holding earnestly the Faith for all time, in all countries, and for all people; and is sent to preach the Gospel to the whole world;
   Apostolic; because it continues steadfastly in the Apostles' teaching and fellowship" (from the Office of Instruction, *Book of Common Prayer*).

6. Pitney Van Dusen, *The Spirit, the Son, and the Father* (New York: Scribner's, 1958).

7. William Barclay, *The Promise of the Spirit,* p. 96.

8. *The Inferno,* Canto XIV, lines 92–93. Appreciation to Professor Michael Campo, Trinity College, Hartford, Conn.

9. See Os Guinness, *The Dust of Death* (Downers Grove, Ill.: Inter-Varisty Press, 1973), chap. 1.

# Key-Word Books for Further Reading

*Conversational Prayer* by Rosalind Rinker. Drops the traditional patterns for prayer and adopts the open language of the heart: honesty, love, simplicity. Provides specific help in learning and teaching how to pray. #91003.

*I Stand by the Door* by Helen Smith Shoemaker. University undergraduates, factory workers, young married couples—all these were, to Sam Shoemaker, special and individual people for whom he poured out all his many talents. Helen Shoemaker's vivid portrait of her husband's life. #4102-4.

*The Secret of Effective Prayer* by Helen Smith Shoemaker. Here is a book which continually affirms the reality of answered prayer. But it does more than that: the author shares with us the "secrets" of praying that she has discovered in her efforts to know God's will. #91004.

*Tracks of a Fellow Struggler* by John R. Claypool. For almost two decades as a pastor, John Claypool participated in the drama of suffering and death—but it was always happening to someone else. But now his own eight-year-old daughter, Laura Lee, was diagnosed as having acute leukemia. John Claypool's personal struggle will help you learn to handle grief in your own life. #91008.

*Ask Me to Dance* by Bruce Larson (#4107-5). Bruce Larson helps you find new ways to look into your heart and the hearts of others in your search for the joy of becoming whole . . . to leave behind a plastic, sterile lifestyle by realizing that there *is* life after rebirth in Christ . . . that it's O.K. to feel deeply and express your feelings.

*Happiness Is Still Homemade* by T. Cecil Myers. How to turn "daylight and dishes" into "moonlight and roses"—all marriage long. Here are tested principles for a happy home life for anyone interested in making marriage more fulfilling and the home more Christian and creative. #91019.

*Living on Tiptoe* by T. Cecil Myers (#4104-0). Shows how by prayer and faith you can improve your own emotional health. Discover how to worry correctly, how to love yourself in the right way, and how to accept positively what cannot be changed.

*Twelfth Man in the Huddle* by David Diles (#4112-1) A galaxy of pro football stars share their thoughts about Jesus Christ. Includes the thoughts of Roger Staubach, Ken Anderson, Lem Barney, Merlin Olsen, and twenty more.

*Parables for Parents and Other Original Sinners* by Tom Mullen. 30 rib-tickling reflections on the realities of parenthood. There's a lot of wisdom mixed in with the wit of these delightful "parables" based on the antics and attitudes of the author's own children. #4100-8.

*Birthdays, Holidays, and Other Disasters* by Tom Mullen (#4105-9). Tom Mullen uses his quick and witty style to take a closer, if somewhat irreverent look at the little events that make up our lives.

*Billy Graham: His Life and Faith* by Gerald Strober (#4116-4). Meet the Billy Graham you probably don't know. His real beliefs, his ambitions, his feelings about Vietnam and Watergate. The real person comes out in Gerald Strober's probing, insightful manuscript.